HEALTH CARE OF A
THOUSAND SLIGHTS

HEALTH CARE OF A THOUSAND SLIGHTS

CONNECTING LEGACY TO ACCESS TO HEALTHCARE

ANJANA SREEDHAR

NEW DEGREE PRESS

HEALTH CARE OF A THOUSAND SLIGHTS

Connecting Legacy to Access to Healthcare

ISBN   978-1-63676-508-2   *Paperback*

978-1-63676-029-2   *Kindle Ebook*

978-1-63676-030-8   *Ebook*

To every person who has ever been slighted by health care—by access, quality, and financial challenges. And to my parents, Geetha and Sreedhar, and my sister, Anushree, for supporting me in my quest to tell these stories—and in everything I do.

To a better world.

CONTENTS

─────

ACKNOWLEDGMENTS

———

My sincerest gratitude to Professor Eric Koester for reaching out to me to join the Book Creators Institute.

I also want to thank my editors—Angela Ivey, Lisa Patterson, and Kendra Kadam—for helping take this book from concept to written piece of work.

I would also like thank my initial developmental editor – Curtis Merritt—for this lovely title idea, and for being on the frontlines of the COVID-19 pandemic as an emergency room physician.

Thank you to the rest of the team at New Degree Press—Brian Bies, Amanda Brown, Gjorgji Pejkovski, Haley Newlin, Lyn Solares, and Jamie T.—for always being open to my questions and for believing I could do this.

Thank you to my incredible family—Geetha Sreedhar, Anushree Sreedhar, and Sreedhar Venkatraman—for supporting me every step of the way. This book would not be here without you supporting my dreams.

Thank you to my incredible partner, Anand, for encouraging me to push the boundaries of what was possible for this book and for all of the articles and advice.

Thank you to one of my best friends I met in DC, Aastha, for cheering me on through late night phone calls and texts of encouragement.

Thank you to my college friends—Bhargavi, Deborah, Jennifer, Kevin, Sidra, and Veronika—for always checking in and for the nudges of support over the past year.

Thank you to my graduate school friends—Dennis, Janelle, and Simone—for reading over my work, providing your thoughts, and sharing your pride and joy with me about this book.

They say you should never forget your roots. For this reason, I have to thank my middle and high school friends—Aswina, Erin, Hongshen, Janice, Nick, Sanyogita, and Yuna—for sharing your excitement of the book with others in your life.

Thanks so much to Tina for supporting my marketing efforts during my preorder book sale.

I would be remiss if I didn't thank those supporting my book journey through preordering and providing feedback on my chapters.

Abhismitha Ramesh, Achchana Ranasinghe, Aisvarya Chandrasekhar, Alexander Moskal, Alexandra Cardinale, Alison Wallach, Allison S Tan, PA-C, Amy Foertsch, Amy

Peterson, Amy Singh, Andre Ware, Andrew Ribe, Andrew Z Dahl, Aneri Parikh, Anna Volski, Annes Kim, Anush Swaminathan, Aparna Sundaram, Arthur Lok, Ashley Petsch, Ashley Sealy, Ashwin Narayan, Aswina Ranasinghe, Audrey Jacobsen, Bedatri Choudhury, Benjamin Jonas, Beth Hightower, Bhargavi Ganesh, Brandon Posivak, Brittany Erskine, Brittany Mazzurco Muscato, Bryan Brown, Byron Zhang, Calandra Branch, Caleb Martin, Camila Romero, Carmen Quinones, Caroline Deng, Chloe Rothbloom, Christie Schweighardt, Coco Lim, Cole Stockton, Courtney Sams, Dakota Pekerti, Dania Khurshid, Daniel Eltes, David Pe Zhao, Devadoss A Subbiah, Devika Balachandran, Divina Li, Dmitriy Zakharov, Dr. Carla Sampson, Emma Johnson, Eric Cova, Eric Song, Esther Kim, Evan Piekara, Fabio I Castelblanco, Frank Jiang, Gayathri Patrachari, Geetha Sreedhar, Giovanni Sanchez, Grace Zhao, Hailey Adler, Hannah Carty, Henggao Cai, Hillary Tsang, Ho Kah Yoke, Jack Amory, Jadayah Spencer, Jane Chen, Jason DuBro, Javon Robinson, Jessica Stolzman, Jeevana Lagisetty, Jeffrey Lu, Jennifer Lu, Jennifer Oh, Jensen Rong, Jessica McCarter, Joan Kao, John Gershman, Jonathan Henry, Jonny Masci, Julia Busto, Julia Ann Mathew, Julie Yelle, Kalikolehua Kellett-Forsyth, Karthik Subramani, Katy Haralson, Kaustubh Deshpande, Kelly Davis, Kevin Li, Konya Badsa, Kristie Fan, Krithika Namasivayam, Kumud R, and Kushaan Shah.

Thanks as well to Laura Waters, Leah Kravets, Lenny Portorreal, Lilian Aluri, Liz Hensler, Logan Jacobs, Loren Dent, Lorraine Venturina, Lotus Buckner, Luis Cisneros, Lynh Nguyen, Maira Undavalli, Manika Harikumar, Marianna Tymocz, Maya Portillo, Megha Madan, Megha Verma, Meghana Laxmidhar Gaopande, Melina Olmo, Michael Dong, Mindy

Wang, Molly Fisch-Friedman, Mutiara Alam, Mythili Vinnakota, Nadeem Farooqi, Neha Kumar, Nicholas Evans, Nicholas Quaglieri, Nikita Bassi, Niranjani Chidamber Papavaritis, Nisha Shankar, Nishil Shah, Nitya Iyer, Olumide Akindutire, Patrick Lin, Patty Medina, Peter Aguilar, Phim Her, Poonam Gupta, Prachi Thapar, Prashanth Vemuganti, Pritam Dodeeja, Priya Gandhi, Priyanka Surio, Radhika Raman, Raishme Singh, Raj Singh, Rangasri Ramji, Reshma Parikh, Rita Wang, Rohan Varshney, Ryan P. Conner, Sahana Arya, Sam Wise, Samantha Martinez, Samir Goel, Samuel Jewett, Sara Zeimer, Sarah Torosyan, Savannah Romero, Seth Ranasinghe, Shashank RK, Shelly Mei, Simone Shaheen, Simran Khadka, Soltan A Bryce, Sonia Rhodes, The Experience Lab, Soumya S. Iyer, Sruthi Narayanan, Stan Rosenberg, Stephanie Greear, Steve Miranda, Sudeep Pisipaty, Sugandha Gupta, Sumi Naidoo, Sushant Thomas, Susmitha Ganagoni, Swati Patel, Sweta Kondapalli, Tania Makker, Tiffany Kang, Troy Costa, Ursula Pawlowski, Vasana N Ranasinghe, Vasudevan Raghavan, Veronika Gadow, Vighnesh Krishnan, Vish Padnani, Weanne Estrada, Will Vogelgesang, Willie Nwanguma, Yamini Vyas, Yolanda Rayside, and Zahra Khetani.

INTRODUCTION

—

Contrasts can, on occasion, be wonderful things. Sandy beaches and hilly mountains. The exuberance of a sunny morning and the reflection that a rainy afternoon brings. The burst of adrenaline you get when you hear a fast song and the calm stillness soft piano tunes can bring.

But some contrasts can be stark—even tragic.

One example of a tragic contrast: In a recent conversation I had with a friend of mine, she shared that she used to work at a federally qualified health center (FQHC) managing health programs in East Oakland, California. East Oakland is comprised predominantly of communities of color. FQHCs are explicitly designed to provide care for the most socially and financially vulnerable patients, who are often uninsured or underinsured. The patients my friend was working with were mostly people of color from low-income backgrounds with a variety of chronic issues and social challenges. One day on her way to work, my friend, who lived in the San Leandro, a community to the southeast of East Oakland, experienced a stark visual contrast.

Standing at the intersection of East Oakland and San Leandro, she noticed something. She told me, "When I faced San Leandro, there's trees lining up the streets, the concrete is paved, and there's lots of mom and pop shops everywhere. To my left, I saw roads that were cracked and no trees anywhere. Lots of closed up and shuttered stores." The contrast was striking.

In that moment, she realized why her patients in East Oakland were facing the health challenges they were facing.

It was because of this contrast in environmental conditions—bringing up larger issues of access to quality care and better quality of life.

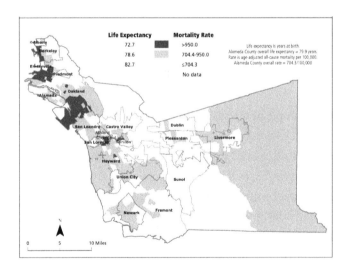

Source: Alameda County vital statistics, 2001-2005.[1]
As this map indicates, mortality rates between East Oakland and San Leandro draw stark contrasts.

---

1   Alameda County Public Health Department. "Alameda County Health Outcomes Report."

While this scene may paint a scary and hopeless situation, this intersection is symbolic of a lot more than the haves and the have nots. After hearing her story, I set out to see if she was standing at the intersection of fear because of lack of access or potential for change.

***

The intersection where my friend stood is indicative of the current health care equity landscape: in some cases, inspiring less hope and more fear. Health disparities continue to persist among marginalized communities—predominantly communities of color, the LGBTQ+ community, women, low-income communities, and those with disabilities—as they continue to suffer with higher prevalence of chronic conditions (like diabetes and hypertension), lower quality of life, and higher mortality rates compared to other Americans.

These contrasts are further described in a damning report from investigative source ProPublica, which revealed that even after accounting for income and other demographic factors, Black women have a much higher maternal mortality rate compared to their white counterparts.[2] For example, a Black woman is "22 percent more likely to die from heart disease than a white woman, 71 percent more likely to perish from cervical cancer, but 243 percent more likely to die from pregnancy or childbirth-related causes." Compared to other countries in the Organization for Economic Cooperation

---

2   Nina Martin, ProPublica, and Renee Montagne, "Nothing Protects Black Women from Dying in Pregnancy and Childbirth," *ProPublica,* December 7, 2017.

and Development (OECD), the United States is far behind in terms of maternal mortality outcomes, placing forty-sixth in the world—far behind its developed counterparts. For Black mothers, these outcomes are further exacerbated. This is partially due to systemic issues of access. Black women are more likely to be uninsured outside of pregnancy, have chronic conditions such as obesity and hypertension, and are more likely to receive lower quality care than white mothers.

These contrasts are not a recent issue and are not just prevalent among communities of color.

In the 1980s, an unnerving disease began spreading in several major cities among young gay men.[3] This disease was later called human immunodeficiency virus (HIV), which can eventually evolve to acquired immunodeficiency syndrome (AIDS). Young gay men were left defenseless, with no response from the federal government. Eventually, activist groups such as ACT UP rallied for more attention on the issue.[4] A few years later, a young boy with hemophilia named Ryan White was diagnosed with the disease after receiving a blood transfusion. The framing around White's youth and his lack of association with the LGBTQ+ community made it socially acceptable for the federal government, which until that point had never mentioned AIDS in press conferences, to take action.

Rewinding further back in time to the early twentieth century, we can also see how some of our country's earliest

---

3   "HIV and AIDS: An Origin Story," Public Health, April 4, 2020.
4   Tim Fitzsimmons, "LGBTQ History Month: The early days of America's AIDS crisis," NBC News, October 15, 2018.

immigrants were also highly limited both in their access to high-quality health care and in their ability to lead healthy lives. As immigrants from eastern Europe came in large numbers to New York City, they had no choice but to live in crowded apartments known as tenements.[5] Apartments and houses designed for single families were rapidly expanded, using cheap materials to fit as many people as possible. Workplaces for immigrants weren't much better; workers were often made to toil for hours in factories that paid them exceedingly minimal wages, the newest Americans of all ages—children included—were subject to occupational hazards because of their living and working environments. This is not unique to the immigrants of the past; current low-income immigrants are often housed in squalid, cramped conditions and work in jobs that provide no bathroom breaks or other basic benefits.

With these examples, it has been easy to collectively blame and shame Black mothers, LGBTQ+ community members, and immigrants—among others—for their health outcomes. We have all heard the comments:

"Well if they don't want diabetes, they need to eat healthier! Why eat junk food all the time?"

"If they weren't so lazy, they'd be in better shape."

While it's easy for our society to pass off these comments as inconsequential, comments like these are simply not true.

---

5   Madison Horne, "Photos Reveal Shocking Conditions of Tenement Slums in the Late 1800s," *History Channel,* January 22, 2020.

It is critical to recognize these comments come from somewhere, from a place of stereotyping, presupposed assumptions, and bias based in opinion, not fact.

These biases lead to a health care delivery system that looks very different for America's marginalized communities—one in which they receive health care of a thousand slights, or moments of disrespect and degradation. The slights can be very small, such as being mixed up with another person of the same racial background at the doctor's office, and can span just a few minutes of awkward interaction. Others are perhaps far bigger than slights; the indigenous community's inability to access health care because of poor public transportation from the legacy of forced relocation to remote areas, for example. For marginalized communities in the United States, these slights—a result of these oppressive legacies—add up over time.

Typically, when something does not work effectively—especially if it's not effective for a large chunk of people—some may argue that "thing" is broken. One argument says these poorer health outcomes in marginalized communities are due to a broken system. But it's necessary to challenge that further by saying that current social systems supporting access to food, transportation, and economic opportunity, as well as land use and more, were intentionally designed to propagate quality of life disparities and support the misguided notion that only some—especially white, straight men—deserve the very best. Once we understand the intentionality of these designs and the essential flaws that come with them, we can better find a way to design policies and programs that undo the impacts of these intentions.

Undoing these impacts is not easy, but I know there is a community in the United States dedicated to making radical changes to our current system.

I am personally invested in developing innovative solutions to overcome health challenges. As an immigrant and, especially as a child of immigrants, I was quick to observe wealth and lifestyle disparities. Our working-class neighborhood in Queens wasn't as glitzy as the touristy neighborhoods in Manhattan we would visit on occasion. When we first moved to New York City as a family, we would treat ourselves once a month to subway trips to Midtown, where we would walk past tall buildings, beautiful parks, and impressive statues. I would wonder what my life would be like if I got to live in a place like Park Avenue—I would have my own room and never have to worry about asking my parents for money. The world would be at my fingertips, ready for the taking. After those jaunts around wealthier neighborhoods, we would go back to Queens and back to our lives.

The contrast felt palpable.

After moving to a fairly affluent, predominantly Asian suburb in New Jersey, it felt as if those differences just vanished. In high school, I discovered the feminist movement and began reading works by Betty Friedan and Gloria Steinem. My understanding of identity dramatically changed when I went off to college, where I slowly discovered not only the works of Black activists and organizers, but those of South and East Asians as well. I learned through my studies, campus activism, and internship experience about how systems were intentionally designed to lock out certain communities.

Federal and local policies such as segregation, migrant worker exploitation, and interning communities like the Japanese during World War II all resulted in long-term discrimination.

The system I have become most interested in is health care provision in the United States. There has been so much well-publicized research on how racism and discrimination have impacted housing, education, access to clean water and air, and many more public services. I have only heard these stories in bits and pieces, so I want to bring those pieces together for people who are dedicated to serving and working with patients. A statement that stayed with me from my first job after getting my bachelor's degree was, "If a child can access excellent education and health care, their quality of life can be leaps and bounds better than that of their parents." As such, I was deeply interested in exploring the connections between historical policy and health care.

Given my internships and two years of work experience in health care research and marketing, I have also experienced a certain uneasiness among health care professionals to discuss health disparities from an honest, frank perspective. My peers are uncomfortable talking about the impact of a phenomenon like the Tuskegee Experiment (which allowed doctors to observe syphilis in low-income Black men, but resulted in the same men not being treated for their disease after the discovery of penicillin) has on health care delivery and patient perception of health care. That discomfort was rooted in the story we tell ourselves about the American narrative, that everyone in this country has a "fair chance" at everything.

Often missing from conversations about health care is how intersections of identity can ultimately impact access. While the term "intersectionality" with respect to identity was originally coined by law professor and academic Kimberlé Crenshaw, it has serious implications for people's lived experiences. BIPOC (Black, Indigenous, and People of Color) experience racism and discrimination. If a person of color also identifies as queer or transgender, their experience is not the same as those who do not; they have to contend with how their queer or trans identity impacts their lived experience.

And that, of course, impacts their ability to access health care and the kinds of health outcomes they could expect.

With the goal of bringing radical change to the forefront of the health care system in mind, I seek to explain the path forward to lessen the disparities in health outcomes. For those just starting to learn about health disparities, I hope for the book to teach the concepts of social determinants of health (non-health factors that impact health), population health (supporting the health of communities), and others. While Americans of means can access oases of health—safe neighborhoods, fitness classes, and easy access to health care services among other things—there are marginalized communities in America located in "health deserts." Because of life circumstances and systematic oppression, the social services needed to support thriving lives is nowhere to be found for them. What is most striking about these contrasts is that they are both seen and unseen. They may be vividly seen at the intersection where my friend stood, or they may be hidden when we stand in line to get dollar cups of coffee at 7/11. I seek to ensure we can bravely identify these contrasts and support marginalized communities in carving out those oases of health care for those in health deserts.

For policymakers, I hope to address how a variety of social issues come together to impact a person's health outcomes. For too long, policy has been made operating in a vacuum, without considering the people involved; only when someone's food, housing, and job needs are met can they truly achieve proper health care. For community advocates who are continuing to fight on behalf of those whom they serve, I hope to highlight their work and provide a broader understanding of how to push against systematic policies that have contributed to discrimination and despair.

***

While on the journey of finding and documenting exciting solutions mitigating health disparities, I had numerous opportunities for interesting and insightful conversations. Some of the key themes that emerged include:

- *Integrating services to improve health is possible.* Despite the obstacles that our society is up against to improve health care outcomes, it is possible to do so by connecting and integrating organizations and sectors that support different aspects of people's health through health care coordination and leveraging technology.
- *Working across sectors to improve health is possible.* Innovative concepts such as design thinking or public-private partnerships are not exclusive to the glitzy worlds of Silicon Valley. We can find small ways to innovate in the

community-based organizations that are committed to supporting the growth and flourishing of marginalized communities.

- *Providing culturally competent care is possible.* By recognizing the true roots of health disparity—discriminatory policy intentionally designed to thwart high quality of life for marginalized communities—we can better understand the path forward.

These solutions can help reduce the contrasts between the haves and the have nots. While the basis of a capitalist society is that inequalities will persist, these solutions can at least aim to reduce them. These solutions can also better uncover where the health care of a thousand slights is taking place and how to stop it from continuing. The policies and programs that can ensure the health and dignity of each American life may not be easy to implement, but we know they are necessary and financially sustainable in the long run.

PART ONE

THOSE WHO WERE FIRST

CHAPTER 1

THE FIRST PEOPLE: THE NATIVE JOURNEY TO HEALTH CARE ACCESS

———

"The ground on which we stand is sacred ground. It is the blood of our ancestors."
—CHIEF PLENTY COUPS, CROW TRIBE

History matters.

As Americans, we often point to moments in our history of which we are most proud: achieving independence from the British (at the time, the most powerful empire in the world), inviting immigrants in to create a melting pot, supporting our World War II veterans with the GI Bill so they, too, could obtain higher education and housing as part of the American Dream, and achieving powerful civil rights milestones.

However, we have many painful memories, too.

The Trail of Tears: forcing hundreds of thousands of Native Americans from their ancestral lands. Slavery: brutalizing and oppressing generations of Black people. The Chinese Exclusion Act: the only piece of legislation to explicitly ban people from a particular country emigrating to the United States. The force-feeding of suffragettes, who worked tirelessly to ensure women could have the right to vote. The Black women who were pushed aside in that same movement. The millions of young lives lost from the HIV/AIDS crisis.

And the list goes on.

It is true these events were all a part of our history. They all happened in our nation's past. What is critical to note, however, is that the legacy of these historical events continues to persist.

Centuries of pushing Native Americans out of their ancestral homes and into reservations without adequate housing or education has resulted in Native Americans having the lowest life expectancy compared to other races.[6] Segregated hospitals in the South ensured the creation of an almost separate nation within the United States, one where citizens had no access to clean water, safe housing, or adequate health care, the impacts of which are continuing to be felt today.[7] Men dominating the medical field for decades has resulted in a lack of studying of chronic conditions that impact women, women not being included in NIH-funded studies about

---

6   Linda Poon, "How 'Indian Relocation' Created a Public Health Crisis," *Bloomberg CityLab,* December 2, 2019.

7   "Power to Heal," directed by Charles Burnett (2018), accessed online.

health and well-being, and women not being taken seriously when describing pain to their physicians.[8]

What is critical to point out here is the historical trends that have allowed for poor health outcomes are not necessarily health specific. For example, the zip code of where someone lives tells us a lot about what resources they have access to. Those resources ultimately determine the choices they are able to make to improve their lives; for example, certain zip codes have higher property values, often meaning better public schools and better public services (transportation, sanitation work, etc.) which ultimately results in better quality of life.

According to Dr. Benjamin Le Cook, director of the Health Equity Research Lab at Harvard Medical School, understanding how neighborhoods can be a window into health outcomes is critical to recognizing their impact. While specific to addiction services, a paper published by Drs. Benjamin Le Cook, Michael Flores, and colleagues outlines the four ways neighborhoods affect health[9]:

- **Access to economic opportunities:** Lower-income communities typically face challenges accessing quality schooling and employment. Public schooling suffers because of the United States' tax-based method of funding public schooling, distinctly putting lower-income

---

8   Jenara Nerenberg. "How to Address Gender Inequality in Health Care," *Greater Good Magazine,* March 9, 2018.

9   Michael Williams Flores et al., "Associations between neighborhood-level factors and opioid-related mortality: A multi--level analysis using death certificate data," *Addiction.* (Feb 2020): 1 - 12.

communities at a disadvantage. Moreover, lower-income communities of color are more likely be located near highways and factories. Highways may serve as a method to isolate people—especially those with limited transport options—from economic opportunities. Living near factories or waste plants increases exposure to pollution, resulting in increased prevalence of conditions like asthma and chronic diabetes.

- **Built environment:** The environments in which these communities exist can exacerbate health disparities. As previously stated, where factories are located says a lot about the health care of the communities that live near them. Moreover, communities that exist near highways, factories, and waste plants may not have exposure to green space, thereby limiting outdoor space to use for exercise. Another part of the built environment also includes measures of safety. If communities are living in fear of increased police activity or general community violence, this has a negative impact on their health as well.

- **Psychosocial factors:** According to this paper, "psychosocial factors can be defined as the influence of social relationships and perceived social control on health outcomes." In communities facing high levels of stress—lack of economic opportunity, lack of access to high-quality social services (like public space, education, and health care), and deterioration of community building and ties—there is a perceived lack of control over many aspects of life. This makes trying to access health care—and overcoming addiction, which is the main point this paper is making—much more challenging.

- **Health care:** The above factors reveal this fact—neighborhoods that have higher densities of Black/Latine (the more gender-inclusive term for people who trace their heritage to Latin America) people have poorer health outcomes. Hospitals that treat Black and Latine people are less likely to have board-certified doctors, as well as doctors who are unable to refer to specialists who are not in the emergency department. This has especially been true during the COVID-19 pandemic, in which already-resource-scarce hospitals serving minority populations—typically more reliant on Medicare/Medicaid monies and other public funds—struggled even further.

***

In some cases, the legacy of these historical events has resulted in certain communities being forced out of our collective memories. These communities have not had the opportunity to select how and where they wanted to build their neighborhoods. This is what has happened with Native Americans in much of our nation.

For centuries in the United States, there have been rules about who is allowed to live where. Sometimes, agreements and treaties made between the federal government and certain groups went unchecked, allowing for the federal government to control the movement of certain populations. A specific example of this is the federal trust responsibility, which was first written about by America's first Supreme Court Chief Justice, John Marshall.[10] Formally codified in 1942, the federal trust responsibility means:

---

10 "Federal Trust Responsibility," U.S. Federal Emergency Management Agency.

"The United States has charged itself
with moral obligations of the highest
responsibility and trust toward Indian tribes."

Most importantly, the federal trust responsibility is not just a
vague set of expectations; it is considered a legally enforceable
fiduciary responsibility of the federal government toward
Native American tribes. Bolstered by language from Supreme
Court cases, the federal government is responsible for protecting tribal lands, treaties, and rights as well as carrying
out mandates of federal law among American Indian and
Alaska Native communities.

Despite the existence of such a documented responsibility,
we can find evidence of the violation of this responsibility
as far back as the nineteenth century through the Trail of
Tears. The Bureau of Indian Affairs was created in 1824, just a
few years before the Trail of Tears formally occurred.[11] After
the passage of the 1830 Indian Removal Act by Congress, the
removal of different Native American nations was deemed
federally necessary, forcing hundreds of thousands to leave
their ancestral lands in search of new homes.[12] Many thousands perished from hunger, thirst, and exhaustion along the
way. This displacement has been seared into the collective
trauma of Native American communities.

Some twenty years later, Congress signed the Indian Appropriations Act, formally creating the Native American reser-

---

11   "Bureau of Indian Affairs," U.S. Department of the Interior: Indian Affairs.
12   "History & Culture," National Park Service.

vation system.[13] This allowed for different nations to be given land for farming and living purposes, but severely curtailed typical Native American practices of hunting, fishing, and food gathering. In most cases, Native Americans were not allowed to leave the reservation without permission. Persistent underinvestment in reservations resulted in increased illness, starvation, and depression among community members.

What has also exacerbated outcomes is that reservations are typically located in food deserts, which makes it challenging to access healthy food. Today, Native community members who are on reservations, around 20 percent of the total Native American population, live in substandard housing and often do not have access to clean, running water.[14,15]

The unrelenting injustice continued. Later in the nineteenth century and well into the twentieth, the federal government began creating Native American boarding schools.[16] Forcefully separating children from parents, boarding schools were intended to "assimilate" Indigenous children into white American culture. They were forced to speak English, wear American-style clothing and hairstyles, and abandon their religious practices in favor of Christianity. Many did not return home because of neglect, lack of food, scarce medical

13   Sarah K. Elliott, "How American Indian Reservations Came to Be," *PBS*, May 25, 2015.

14   Joe Whittle, "Most Native Americans live in cities, not reservations. Here are their stories," *The Guardian*, September 4, 2017.

15   Laurel Morales, "Many Native Americans Can't Get Clean Water, Report Finds," *NPR*, November 18, 2019.

16   Sarah K. Elliott, "How American Indian Reservations Came to Be," *PBS*, May 25, 2015.

care, and rampant sexual abuse. For the ones who did come back home, it became yet another collective trauma seared into the memories of Native American communities. This trauma has gradually become inter-generational in nature, with those who were forced to go to boarding schools now serving as elders in Indian country. Since those then-children were never lovingly parented, it became increasingly challenging for them to ensure they were able to adequately parent their own children.

Forcing Native American children to separate and requiring Native American communities to keep relocating did not stop in the nineteenth century. While the creation of the Bureau of Indian Affairs occurred in 1824, as recently as 1956, Congress passed the Indian Relocation Act, which dissolved federal recognition of certain tribes and ended federal funding for much-needed social services on reservations, such as schools and hospitals.

The primary intention behind the Act was to encourage Native American families to leave their reservations and "assimilate" by living in cities. Despite this encouragement, there was little done to provide job training and prevent rampant job discrimination that kept Native Americans disconnected from their communities and in poverty. According to former Indian Affairs Commissioner Phileo Nash, the unmet promises around job training ensured a "one-way ticket from rural to urban poverty."[17]

---

17   Alexia Fernandez Campbell, "How America's Past Shapes Native Americans' Present," *The Atlantic*, October 12, 2016.

These forced relocations and attempts at assimilation have had profound, multigenerational impacts on the health care that Native Americans have access to and receive. According to health care researcher and Ojibwe tribe member Dr. Melissa Walls, Ojibwe tribe members engaged in something called a "seasonal round" when they were living together.[18] The seasonal round occurred when each new season brought new sources of food, the process of obtaining these resulting in a loss of a lot of calories. By shifting to government-sponsored commodity programs, Native Americans began relying on commodity goods—flour, sugar, lard, and butter—which caused increases in obesity. One of the foods that has become central to Native American culture and life is frybread, which is essentially fried dough.[19] Frybread become a symbol of Native pride and unity, but is also a painful reminder of how forced relocation required Native communities to give up their traditional ways of gathering and obtaining healthy foods.

Most importantly, these increases in obesity have persisted generationally. According to a paper published by Walls and her colleagues, "families who've gone through those relocation programs have the worst health outcomes that we can track across three generations."[20] Given the immense

---

18 Linda Poon, "How 'Indian Relocation' Created a Public Health Crisis," *Bloomberg CityLab,* December 2, 2019.

19 Jen Miller, "Frybread," *Smithsonian Magazine,* July 2008.

20 Melissa Walls and Les B. Whitebeck, "The Intergenerational Effects of Relocation Policies on Indigenous Families," *Journal of Family Issues,* June 14, 2012.

communal pain those who have been forced to relocate experience, the fact that American Indians/Alaska Natives experience PTSD more than twice as often as the general population should not be surprising. Native Americans are also far more likely to use and abuse drugs and alcohol at younger ages compared to the rest of the population.[21]

While frybread is considered a staple in most Native diets, it is also a reminder of past food practices that had to be abandoned due to forced relocation.
Source: Flickr[22]

Spirited Dr. Melissa Walls is no stranger to the lives of those she studies. As an Ojibwe tribe member, she has rooted her research and scholarship in her personal background and experience. She has seen close family members pass away from complications related to type 2 diabetes. Growing up in

21   Editorial Staff, "Rise of Alcoholism Among Native Americans," *American Addiction Centers,* January 2, 2020.

22   Lou Stejskal (loustejskal), "Aged Cheddar Rillettes—Truffle, cauliflower, fry bread," Flickr photo, December 2, 2017.

a Native American family that lived outside of a reservation, she recalls having to visit the nearest reservation to access any medical or dental care. Poignantly, Walls stated, "When you grow up in that context, you don't label it as an inequity or disparity. It's just sort of your reality."[23]

At the suggestion of an uncle who served as a liaison between academic and local tribe communities, Walls began studying Native health in graduate school. Walls gained national prominence after defending her dissertation on mental health and suicide in Indigenous youth in 2007. Walls has since become a leader in Native American health research, codirecting the Research for Indigenous Community Health Center at the University of Minnesota College of Pharmacy and most recently as the director of the Great Lakes Hub for the Center for American Indian Health from the Johns Hopkins Bloomberg School of Public Health.[24, 25]

Health care access among Native American communities has a history as storied as relocation. The Indian Health Service (IHS), the program through which Native Americans had access to health care, was developed after the establishment of the Bureau of Indian Affairs.[26] After the IHS was transitioned to the US Public Health Service—under the Department of

23 Linda Poon, "How 'Indian Relocation' Created a Public Health Crisis," *Bloomberg CityLab,* December 2, 2019.

24 "Melissa Walls Ph.D. and Michelle Johnson-Jennings Ph.D. Discuss Historical Trauma," Dodging Bullets, accessed March 23, 2020.

25 "Melissa Walls," Johns Hopkins Bloomberg School of Public Health Center for American Indian Health, accessed on March 24, 2020.

26 Donald Warne, MD and Linda Bane Frizzell, PhD, "American Indian Health Policy: Historical Trends and Contemporary Issues," *American Journal of Public Health* 104, no. S3 (2014): S263 - S267.

Health & Human Services—health care provision continued, albeit under continued underfunding. For Native American communities, trusting the federal government with another important provision continues to be a challenge.

The New York Times shares a damning story of an IHS facility, Sioux San, in western South Dakota, which closed down because of inability to provide adequate care.[27] The closure of the facility limited Native American access to health care in that region, especially because any care received at a private hospital/clinic would not be covered by IHS, resulting in thousands of dollars in potential out-of-pocket costs. In this respect, according to Rear Admiral Michael Weahkee of the IHS (and the Zuni tribe), "I don't think the federal government has fulfilled its treaty obligations for providing health care because it has not provided IHS with the resources to do so."

It is not surprising for many Native Americans to know the IHS is chronically underfunded. Despite rumors that Native Americans receive free health care through the federal government, the IHS is similar to the Veterans Health Administration in its function: it is responsible for running clinics and hospitals where members can obtain care. The funding for the IHS, however, remains woefully inadequate; in 2016, Congress allocated $4.8 billion to the IHS budget. Spread out across 3.7 million Native Americans and Alaska Natives, the spending comes out to less than $2,000 per person.[28]

---

27 Mark Walker, "Fed Up With Deaths, Native Americans Want to Run Their Own Health Care," *New York Times,* October 15, 2019.

28 Mark Walker, "Fed Up With Deaths, Native Americans Want to Run Their Own Health Care," *New York Times,* October 15, 2019.

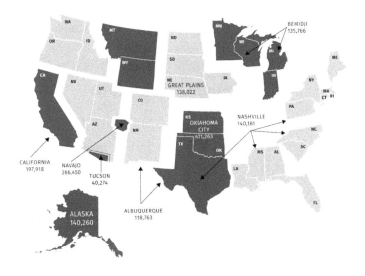

This graphic shows the patient populations in each service area for the Indian Health Service.
Source: Government Accountability Office, Wikipedia Images[29]

Now, however, more and more tribes are looking to take control over health care facilities. For example, the Alaska Native Tribal Health Consortium, a nonprofit established by Alaska Native leaders, has found success in partnering with Veterans Affairs to expand Native American health care access to veterans' facilities.[30] They have been able to stay financially sustainable by aggressively pursuing grant funding, billing through the Center for Medicare and Medicaid Services, and using money from the casino industry.

29 U.S. Government Accountability Office, "Figure 1: Indian Health Service Patient Population by Area, Calendar Year 2014," Wikipedia images, January 23, 2017.

30 Alaska Native Tribal Health Consortium, "Overview," accessed on March 27, 2020.

However, for smaller tribes that cannot rely on casinos as a source of income, taking control of health care is much more challenging.

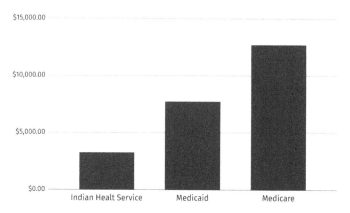

Per Patient Spend, 2017

Comparing patient spend across IHS, Medicaid, and Medicare.
Source: *The New York Times*[31]

It is also essential to point out federal organizations such as the Bureau of Indian Affairs and the Indian Health Service are only accessible to federally recognized tribes. If you come from a state-only recognized tribe in North Carolina, for example, you do not have access to these services. For smaller, more localized tribes, this has meant having to find other ways to provide for and protect community members. According to *NPR*, private health care systems often don't know how to care for Native American patients because of the challenges these patients have in accessing private insurance.[32]

---

31 Ibid.
32 Eric Whitney, "Native Americans Feel Invisible in US Health Care System," *NPR from Montana Public Radio*, December 12, 2017.

Only those who are able to get monetary support from tribe members are able to access care that isn't covered by the IHS or won't be covered by the IHS because of lack of federal recognition.

For centuries, Native Americans have been let down by the federal government with respect to the federal trust responsibility. Instead of honoring treaties and previous commitments, the federal government has historically underfunded and actively harmed Native American communities and their well-being. This has naturally resulted in a deep mistrust of non-Native institutions, such as the federal and state governments, public schools, and hospitals.

In order to restore that trust, my friend Logan Jacobs, who identifies with a state-recognized tribe in North Carolina, mentioned the need for the federal government to more closely listen to and understand community needs, rather than entering communities and telling them what to do. Her advice is reminiscent of the concept of the "white savior complex." The white savior complex occurs when a white individual acts to help non-white communities without fully understanding or listening to their needs; in some cases, the helper may not even center the community they are seeking to help in their work.

While often used in international aid/relief contexts, this behavior also accurately describes how the federal government has treated Native American communities. The white savior complex has become so well-known that it has been parodied by a Barbie Savior Instagram account.[33] The account includes sarcastic captions on pictures of a white Barbie doll teaching children in Africa, performing "exotic dances" with community members, and more.

In fact, the white savior complex is the best way to explain how the American government approached interacting with Indigenous communities in the United States. Intervening in Indigenous communities by taking children away from their parents and societies—thinking their families would be unable to raise them—is a primary example of not understanding community needs.

By contrast, the idea of supporting by listening to what a community requires can better ensure resource allocation occurs at the nexus of community well-being and need.

***

In the meantime, a few promising solutions to address health challenges in Native communities have come to the fore.

An IHS health program that runs on a shoestring budget of $100 million has also started to see important gains in health care outcomes. The Special Diabetes Program for Indians (SDPI) deploys grants to IHS, tribal, and urban health programs to enhance local diabetes treatment.[34] By providing

33 Damian Zane, "Barbie challenges the 'white saviour complex,'" *BBC*, April 30, 2016.

34 Indian Health Service, "Special Diabetes Program for Indians (SDPI)," accessed on April 2, 2020.

funding directly to tribal leadership, community members are able to better manage and prevent diabetes and cardiovascular disease. Indeed, a 2014 randomized controlled trial established a lifestyle intervention group and a placebo group.[35] Through lifestyle intervention efforts and tribe-led intensive case management, the trial achieved a 58 percent reduction in diabetes incidence compared to the placebo group. Through seventeen years of SDPI funding, health outcomes have gradually improved, resulting in increased services and decreased average blood sugar, LDL cholesterol, and blood pressure.

Partners in Health (PIH), a Boston-based nonprofit that supports health care delivery nationally and globally, also partners with tribes in Indian country to improve health care access. One such example is the Community Outreach and Patient Empowerment (COPE) program, which PIH started when invited to work with the Navajo Nation's health system in 2009.[36] COPE is comprised of two key initiatives: developing a community health representatives program and combatting diabetes.

- Through receiving training in nursing assistance, community health representatives build trust with Navajo Nation tribe members by helping them access resources, attend prenatal appointments, and manage chronic

35 U.S. Department of the Interior, Bureau of Indian Affairs, Indian Health Service, *Special Diabetes Program for Indians 2014 Report to Congress: Changing the Course of Diabetes: Turning Hope into Reality,* (Washington DC, 2014), 1-10.

36 Partners in Health, "Navajo Nation: PIH serves Native Americans struggling with some of the worst health outcomes in the United States," accessed on April 2, 2020.

conditions. Community health representatives also ensure that patient materials are easily accessible for community members who do not speak English as a first language and conduct workshops to raise patient awareness.

- The Navajo Nation has only thirteen grocery stores in an area the size of West Virginia, resulting in easy access to junk food and challenges in obtaining healthier foods. Through the Navajo Fruit & Vegetable Prescription Program (FVRx), doctors prescribe fruits and vegetables to overweight families, giving them vouchers for free produce. Through small local shops, Navajo families are able to use the vouchers to obtain fresh groceries. The FVRx program has allowed nearly a third of initially overweight children to meet the criteria for healthy weight.

SDPI is an example of what is possible in Indian country when evidence-based research and strategies are deployed by those who know and understand their community members. Moreover, according to health researcher and Ojibwe tribe member Melissa Walls, not all is lost in Native American communities.[37]

While the overall narrative of communal trauma and being forgotten persists, Walls points out that Native American communities struggle with inequities, "but also have vibrant and cultural richness, family-centric [communities] with communal, take-care-of-one-another thinking." Community

---

37   Linda Poon, "How 'Indian Relocation' Created a Public Health Crisis," *Bloomberg CityLab,* December 2, 2019.

support is critical for Native American tribes, and they need to be further bolstered by robust social services that can support their daily needs. While Native American history matters, so does the present and future of community members' well-being.

CHAPTER 2

WE SHALL OVERCOME: THE ONGOING BATTLE FOR HEALTH CARE ACCESS IN THE BLACK COMMUNITY

———

"Of all the forms of inequality, injustice in health care is the most shocking and inhumane."
—DR. MARTIN LUTHER KING JR., CIVIL RIGHTS LEADER

Upon studying the health of Black enslaved people and their descendants in the eighteenth to twentieth centuries, white physicians believed one thing: all questions about health could be answered by the body. If members of the Black community had poorer health outcomes, it was due to racial weaknesses, not socioeconomic situations.[38]

Conclusions drawn from past studies indicate the same. In the 1700s, when yellow fever hit white communities harder than Black ones, physicians assumed that Black people were immune to the disease because of their race. Perhaps these same assumptions allowed for persistent rumors about COVID-19 not affecting Black people, spreading serious disinformation among the Black community.[39] These rumors have unfortunately been spread by members of the Black community on social media, making taking COVID-19 seriously even more challenging.

When enslaved people suffered from poor health—which was common, considering lack of access to nutritious food and safe working conditions—their treatment and healing were contingent on ensuring they would still be able to work. Ailments that didn't seriously affect their ability to work, such as colds, were considered negligible, so nothing was done to provide proper care—or even preventive care. With that being the case, enslaved Black people were more likely to suffer from respiratory infections from poor housing conditions.

Enslaved people were routinely subject to random experimentation in medication dosages and spontaneous surgery, making physicians complicit in inflicting egregious harm on them. Care for enslaved people was highly dependent

---

38 Stanford School of Medicine Ethnogeriatrics, "Health history: Up from Slavery," accessed on April 7, 2020.

39 Aleem Maqbool, "Coronavirus: Why has the virus hit African Americans so hard?", *BBC*, April 11, 2020.

on what their masters thought about them. Unfortunately, the level of danger an enslaved person was exposed to was a direct part of his or her owner's commercial calculations.

In some cases, owners would even limit enslaved people's access to care by claiming they were malingering, or pretending to be ill.[40] This was especially true of older, more disabled enslaved people, who were no longer valuable in the fields or as "breeders" to produce more enslaved people.

As such, caring for elderly, disabled enslaved people became tenuous, often resulting in them being told to peddle or beg to pay for themselves.[41]

This "slave health deficit" continues to drive current health care disparities between Black and white Americans.[42] Indeed, every part of the slave trade is marked with health hazards and high death rates. Starting with "the interior trek, the middle passage, the breaking in period, and the enslavement," this health disparity has not been alleviated despite the efforts made to make things more equal during Reconstruction and the civil rights movement.

***

40 Harriet A. Washington, "First Chapter: Medical Apartheid," *The New York Times*, February 18. 2007.

41 Stanford School of Medicine Ethnogeriatrics, "Health history: Up from Slavery," accessed on April 7, 2020.

42 Vernellia Randall, "Eliminating the Slave Health Deficit: Using Reparation to Repair Black Health," *Poverty & Race* 11, no. 6 (2002): 3-8, 14.

One of the great dangers of social and public policy is the need to reinvent the wheel to solve our society's most critical problems. Those of us who care about social problems may quickly get caught up in the zeitgeist of harnessing the power of technology and associated buzzwords to do something new and innovative.

We may forget—or perhaps, we were never taught—quite a few solutions are already in place, but they are not widely used. So many contributions have already been made in alleviating social ills but may not be fully recognized or appreciated. Some of these solutions have involved rigorous scientific research to refute social claims and moving narratives that humanize vulnerable populations.

And that's where W. E. B. DuBois comes in.

With an upturned mustache and a perpetually serious look, W. E. B. DuBois definitely had a lot on his mind as one of the eminent Black intellectuals of his time. He was born shortly after slavery was made illegal in the United States and died just one day before Martin Luther King Jr. gave his famous "I Have a Dream" speech in Washington, D.C. He was the earner of many firsts—the first Black person to earn a PhD at Harvard, the first researcher to use social science to disprove racial theories about Black poverty, and one of the first intellectual contemporaries to challenge a popular rival, Booker T. Washington, on a path to define the place of Black people in American society.

While W. E. B. DuBois enjoyed a happy childhood where he was treated well by Black and white peers alike in

Massachusetts, he began to notice disparities in how Black people were treated while studying at Fisk University in Nashville, Tennessee. After this time, he had the opportunity to earn a master's degree in Berlin, studying alongside some of the most prominent social theorists of the time. His time in Berlin greatly influenced the way he conducted sociological work.

In fact, DuBois made history by using the theories and practices he learned in Berlin when he published *The Philadelphia Negro: A Social Study* in 1899. This study was the first to apply rigorous social science methods to study an often-neglected population: Black people. Known as "Negroes" at the time, they were often blamed for the poverty, crime, and illiteracy that ran rampant in their neighborhoods. DuBois was able to do further study on African Americans by surveying Black families living in the Seventh Ward in Philadelphia. Choosing this part of town was critical to understanding racial dynamics and tensions in the neighborhood, since affluent white families lived on the fringes of the ward alongside Black families from a variety of backgrounds.

By collecting over five thousand surveys and tracking information about household income, health, and information about inhabitants, DuBois was able to use research to tell a convincing tale of diversity and advancement. DuBois first recognized the inner hierarchy that existed among the Black community, recognizing not all Blacks were poor or illiterate. Using some of sociology's first infographics, DuBois was able to prove that "the Negro problem" was ostensibly "not one problem, but rather a plexus of social problems," and had little correlation to the Black "social pathology" than to whites' enforcement of racial discrimination and a provision of unequal opportunity.[43]

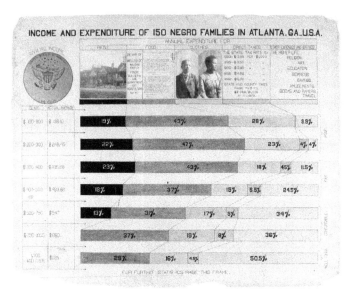

Known for his immaculate hand-drawn graphics, W. E. B. DuBois relied on them to effectively communicate data about Black families' income and health.
Source: The Public Domain[44]

At the turn of the century, DuBois focused his efforts on challenging his intellectual contemporary, Booker T. Washington. Washington, then esteemed in Black elite circles, advocated for Black people to focus on vocational trade as a method of contributing to American society. Washington also argued Black people did not need to be integrated into white society.

---

43 Stephen McGrail, "Philadelphia Negro (The)," *The Encyclopedia of Greater Philadelphia,* accessed on April 9, 2020.

44 Library of Congress, "W.E.B. DuBois' Hand-Drawn Infographics of African-American Life (1900)."

DuBois challenged this perspective, insisting on the need for Black people to have access to the same opportunities as their white peers. To that effect, DuBois cofounded the now-famous National Association for the Advancement of Colored People (NAACP), which fought for integration and civil rights throughout the twentieth century.

In 1909, DuBois slightly veered away from using research as a platform to promote racial equality by publishing *The Souls of Black Folk*. Using quotes from old spiritual songs and hymns sung by former enslaved people in introductions, this book was more autobiographical in nature, drawing from DuBois's personal experiences and the experiences of those in the Black community. In this text, DuBois highlighted the challenges facing Black people in society, terming it "double consciousness."

According to DuBois:

> *"An American, a Negro… two souls, two thoughts, two unreconciled strivings; two warring ideals in one dark body, whose dogged strength alone keeps it from being torn asunder."*

For Black people, they had to learn how to balance not only how they perceived themselves, but how others perceived them because of their salient racial identity.

DuBois has taught our society two key elements: one is that, through rigorous academic research, one can disprove social ills unfairly ascribed to a population. The second, however, is that science and research alone are not enough. *The Souls of Black Folk* sought to highlight for its audience the critical conditions Black people in American society faced and sought to humanize a community otherwise blamed for the challenges it faced.

***

Many negative health challenges that Black women in particular face are also rooted in the evil history of slavery. One cannot talk about the health of enslaved Black women without mentioning Dr. James Marion Sims.[45]

Credited as the father of "modern gynecology," Dr. Sims invented the gynecological speculum, used for examinations, and has contributed to knowledge on how to surgically correct a fistula, a defect that can occur after childbirth. But his knowledge came from experimenting on the bodies of enslaved women. As early as the 1830s, there has been historical evidence of medical experimentation on women's bodies. Dr. Sims began experimenting on enslaved women—three of whom to perfect ovary removal, which is an otherwise very difficult procedure. Purposefully withholding anesthesia from slaves, Sims would enlist fellow male colleagues or

---

45   Ranjani Chakraborty, "The US medical system is still haunted by slavery," *Vox,* December 7, 2017

other enslaved women to restrain the enslaved person he was experimenting on.

A statue of Dr. James Marion Sims in Central Park. Once his experimental practices on Black women came to light, this statue was removed.
Source: Wikipedia[46]

Sims, like many of his time, believed Black people did not feel pain or anxiety like white patients would. This misinformation has continued to dictate quality of care Black patients continue to receive to this day. More importantly, Black patients suffering from pain are chronically undertreated

---

46 Jim Henderson, "Statue of Sims in New York's Central Park, removed in April 2018," Wikipedia images, May 24, 2008.

in the American health care system, especially in the emergency department.

According to author of *Medical Apartheid*, Harriet A. Washington, "What does it mean when you say that someone doesn't feel pain? Among other things, you're speaking about their humanity. This is part of that suite of beliefs emanating from the nineteenth century that we have still not shaken off, despite all our knowledge and sophistication. They're deeply ingrained."[47]

The medical system continued to target Black women as waves of immigrants came to the United States in the early twentieth century, sparking the highly racist eugenics movement. Designed to reduce the childbearing potential of the poor and disabled, eugenicists began work on the notorious "Negro Project," which pushed birth control in the Black South. Surprisingly, this project garnered support from the otherwise-radical W. E. B. DuBois, who contended that Blacks were reproducing at a careless rate.

Over time, many states passed pro-sterilization laws, resulting in several instances of forced sterilization. Dubbed the "Mississippi appendectomy," hysterectomies became commonplace among Black female patients—even if they were going in for other procedures. Civil rights activist Fannie Lou Hamer described having gone into the hospital for a tumor removal, but found that doctors had also removed her uterus without consent.[48] This underscores a serious point

---

47 Ranjani Chakraborty, "The US medical system is still haunted by slavery," *Vox*, December 7, 2017.

48 Ibid.

that Harriet Washington brought up in an interview: while the children born to Black women in the past represented economic value, now they represented a burden that the American economic system had to support.

Black maternal death has been on the rise in the United States, according to a damning report from investigative source ProPublica.[49] Even rich women, like tennis star Serena Williams, and well-educated women, like epidemiologist Dr. Shalon Irving, suffered the negative health effects of preexisting conditions and intergenerational stress. For Dr. Irving, this resulted in her tragically dying three weeks after giving birth to her daughter at age thirty-six. It is clear that these maternal and neonatal health outcomes for Black families are not uncommon; even more so, these outcomes are rooted in an exploitative medical system that has systematically mistreated Black women.

While bodily exploitation may have been rooted in how our medical system has treated Black women, it has now become a strategy to undermine and destroy the dignity of other people of color. A clear example of this is the news from earlier in 2020 about mass hysterectomies performed on women in the detention centers run by US Immigration and Customs Enforcement (ICE).[50]

---

49 Nina Martin, ProPublica, and Renee Montagne, "Nothing Protects Black Women from Dying in Pregnancy and Childbirth," *ProPublica,* December 7, 2017.

50 Rachel Treisman, "Whistleblower Alleges 'Medical Neglect,' Questionable Hysterectomies of ICE Detainees," *NPR,* September 16, 2020.

***

The Black community continued to fight for proper access to health care well into the latter parts of the twentieth century.

"A system of racial segregation dictated every aspect of social life."

Actor Danny Glover's voice narrates the story of ending hospital segregation and improving quality of care for Black people. In the documentary *The Power to Heal*, interviews with doctors and nurses serving in segregated hospitals, civil rights activists, and journalists highlighted the state of health care for millions of Black people in the United States before segregation.[51]

Racial segregation, which began in earnest after the Civil War but was in full force in the era of Jim Crow, resulted in "separate but equal" public institutions. While most of American historical storytelling is focused on places like public parks, buses, and schools, segregation had a direct impact on health care as well. Separate but equal, as defined by Supreme Court case *Plessy v. Ferguson*, did not actually result in equal accommodations.

In order to even get to the hospital, white ambulances would not take Black patients: more often than not, Black patients were taken in hearses that were not being used. Hospitals that

---

51   Power to Heal," directed by Charles Burnett (2018), accessed online.

were willing to admit Black patients were often further away, resulting in some Black patients dying en route to hospitals while being carried in a hearse. Often, hospitals serving Black patients had fewer resources, which resulted in poorer health outcomes. According to Dr. Alvin Pouissant, "Every time you went into a hospital that was segregated, it was saying to you that your life as a Black person was not worth as much as a white life."[52]

Even in hospitals that served both Black and white patients, wards were segregated, with little space given to Black patients. Regardless of condition—whether it was labor and delivery, chemotherapy treatment, or tuberculosis recovery—all Black patients were kept together in the same ward. Services were duplicated and resources—ventilators and blood banks, for example—were kept completely separate. Black patients were often not prioritized in their care, unless Black doctors were at their disposal. Otherwise, dangerous assumptions were made about the kind of care Black patients deserved to receive.

This level of separation was maintained in how clinical workers were trained—many northern schools refused to admit Black medical and nursing students. Black medical graduates struggled to get residency opportunities; outside of Black hospitals like Harlem Hospital in New York City, options were quite limited. Black doctors were not allowed to join the American Medical Association (AMA), not allowed to be members of their local medical societies, and therefore not

---

52 Harvard Medical School Medical Education, "Alvin F. Pouissant, MD," accessed on April 13, 2020.

allowed to admit patients or treat patients in local hospitals. These legal barriers continued to exacerbate health disparities by reducing access to hospitals and medical care.

Moreover, the AMA funded research for The Flexner Report in 1910, designed to reform medical education across the country.[53] By 1923, schools that did not meet the newly designed criteria laid out by the Flexner Report were closed. More importantly, this included the closure of five of seven medical schools for Black students—greatly affecting the future pipeline of Black physicians. These legal barriers continued to exacerbate health disparities by continuing to reduce access to hospitals and medical care.

While some health activists, such as Dorothy Ferebee, helped to structure health outreach programs for vulnerable communities, access to health care continued to be difficult. In many cases, Black communities continued to rely on old herbal remedies passed down through generations.[54]

In fact, the roots of doulas and midwives for expecting Black mothers come from a history of not accessing proper medical care and relying on community knowledge to support the health of mother and baby. Doula services, such as Ancient Song Doula Services in Brooklyn, continue to operate in this tradition.[55]

53 Elizabeth Hlavnika, "Racial Bias in Flexner Report Permeates Medical Education Today," *Medpage Today,* June 18, 2020.

54 AAUW, "Dorothy Celeste Boulding Ferebee Pioneering Civil Rights and Healthcare," accessed on April 15, 2020.

55 Ancient Song Doula Services, "About Us," accessed on April 15, 2020.

As more and more Black doctors were being trained at institutions like historically Black school Howard University in DC or Meharry Medical College in Nashville, Black communities grew increasingly reliant on them. Operating out of their black briefcases, Black doctors would come to people's homes to deliver babies or sew stitches on a wound.

***

The documentary detailed how things changed through policy shifts. In 1946, Congress drafted the Hill-Burton Act, which provided funding for the construction and building of hospitals. This would transform the health care system, especially by providing extra support for already-underfunded Black hospitals and clinics. Some hoped this would be the opportunity to integrate health care facilities. However, in order to get it through the legislative agenda, Southerners insisted on continued segregation of health care facilities. As a result, the Hill-Burton Act was the only piece of legislation from the twentieth century that had "separate but equal" written into it.[56]

Black doctors and other clinicians began to mobilize. Using civil rights as the lens through which they treated their patients and advocated for change, Black doctors formed the National Medical Association in response to the structural racism of not being allowed to be part of the AMA. Black clinicians participated in civil rights marches, including the famous March on Washington. They paid close attention to

---

56   Power to Heal," directed by Charles Burnett (2018), accessed online.

Supreme Court cases such as *Brown v. Board of Education* (1954), recognizing that these hard-fought civil rights could have a significant impact on patient care and health care more broadly.

The pressure was on the American Medical Association to give Black doctors admitting privilege at white hospitals as well as to treat Black doctors better more generally. Despite attempts to partner with AMA on conversations about hospital integration and pushing the AMA to come out unequivocally against segregation, there was still no response.

In Greensboro, North Carolina, dentist George Simkins was trying to push for change in arguably controversial ways. Having already been jailed for trying to integrate a golf course, Dr. Simkins was looking for the support of the NAACP Legal Defense Fund to support Black doctors' admitting privileges at white hospitals in Greensboro. After hearing a story of a pediatric patient who was refused admission to a white hospital because of his race, Dr. Simkins wanted to push on this further. As a dentist, he knew that he had more independence compared to physicians. He, therefore, was able to bring more civil rights issues in medicine to litigation.

Slowly, progress was being made. With Simkins' leadership and support, the NAACP filed a suit against white hospitals outlining that they had been funded through the Hill-Burton Act and should therefore also accept Black patients. While Simkins and company lost in district court, they were noticed by US Attorney General Robert F. Kennedy when they appealed to 4th Circuit Court of Appeals.

Setting a legal precedent, Kennedy was able to enter the decision as a friend on behalf of the plaintiffs, instead of the defendants. Kennedy's involvement allowed for the appeals court to rule in favor of Simkins and company. On November 1, 1963—three weeks before Robert F. Kennedy's brother, President John F. Kennedy, was assassinated—this decision came down, allowing the striking down of the "separate but equal" provision in the Hill-Burton Act.

While this was a great legal breakthrough, it created an additional challenge in terms of enforcement. The only way to enforce the ruling was to sue every segregated hospital in the country for staying segregated, emphasizing the need for more comprehensive legislation. The seminal Civil Rights Act—started under the Kennedy administration and passed under the Johnson administration after much negotiation with southern, anti-integration Democrats—**stipulated that if an institution received federal funds under Title VI, it was not allowed to discriminate on the basis of race.**

However, there was no formal way to enforce this, outside of the Department of Health, Education, and Welfare (HEW)—the forerunner for the Departments of Education and Health & Human Services—attempting to sue every Southern hospital for explicit segregation.

Then, Medicare happened. Before the 1964 election, President Lyndon Johnson wanted to ensure elderly people over the age of sixty-five would be guaranteed health insurance. Despite fierce opposition from the American Medical Association, the National Medical Association's leader, Dr. W. Montague Cobb, testified in favor of the bill. After winning the election,

Johnson was able to ensure Medicare would be supported by the House's Ways and Means Committee.

While elderly Americans were quickly signing up for health care through Medicare, challenges persisted—the funding that would be used to reimburse hospitals for services would support segregated hospitals even still. Under increasing pressure from organizations like the NAACP, HEW created an Office for Civil Rights, which quickly recruited people from the NAACP to start moving toward desegregating hospitals nationally. The goal was to integrate all hospitals across the United States before Medicare was officially implemented in July 1965.

In a true race against time, HEW's seven hundred inspectors—most of whom had no background in health care—went to hospitals across the South to observe facilities and provide recommendations on how to effectively desegregate.[57] Some Southern hospitals would engage in what was then known as the "HEW Shuffle," in which staff would switch beds and chart readings to indicate their facility had integrated in time for inspection. In some cases, inspectors were threatened with violence, threats, and intimidation.

One month before the deadline, 75 percent of hospitals and 50 percent of hospitals in the South had been properly desegregated.[58] During a nationally televised press conference, President Johnson applied pressure to hospital administrators

---

57   Power to Heal," directed by Charles Burnett (2018), accessed online.
58   Ibid.

unwilling to integrate, saying their hospitals would simply receive no funding for treating Medicare patients.

This was the financial and social pressure needed to turn the dial—through the Johnson administration's commitment to Medicare and the Civil Rights Act, and the tireless efforts of civil rights and health care organizations, over 90 percent of all hospitals nationally were successfully desegregated.

While these larger movements were occurring in the macro-context of American history, there were also some gravely somber moments of Black people being mistreated with respect to health care. Most Americans are taught in school about the Tuskegee Experiment.[59] After the Public Health Service gathered six hundred Black men to participate in the study, designed to record the natural history of syphilis, the Public Health Service told participants that that they were being treated for "bad blood," a local term referring to any number of ailments, including fatigue and anemia.

It was discovered in 1972 that the service failed to obtain the participants' informed consent. Perhaps most critically, they did not give patients proper treatment to cure their illness despite penicillin being made available in 1947. While the Tuskegee Experiment is now widely studied in medical ethics classes, it is a clear example of how the Black community has been let down by American medicine.

---

59   U.S. Centers for Disease Control and Prevention, "U.S. Public Health Service Syphilis Study at Tuskegee," accessed on April 16, 2020.

***

What is also incredibly interesting is how health outcomes for Black immigrants—people moving to the United States from Africa and the Caribbean in recent decades—are markedly different compared to their counterparts who can trace their heritage to enslaved people.

According to an article published in the *Journal of Healthcare for the Poor and Underserved*[60]:

> *"This advantage may be due to healthier lifestyles in the countries of origin, selective migration of healthy immigrants, stronger support systems in their home countries or fewer experiences of racialized stress and discrimination."*

However, the longer Black immigrants live in the United States, the more their health outcomes worsen from adopting less healthy practices and losing access to their cultural safety nets.

So, inequalities in health care persist for Black people.

***

---

60 Derek M. Griffith, Jonetta Johnson, Rong Zhang, Harold Neighbors, and James S. Jackson, "Ethnicity, Nativity, and the Health of American Blacks," *Journal of Healthcare for the Poor and Underserved* 22, no.1 (2011): 142-156.

Often, innovative solutions are built on visionary leadership, such as that of W. E. B. DuBois. However, that leadership and vision are not sufficient. Galvanizing others to believe in your vision and using a mix of research and narrative to shift policy and culture is also necessary.

Dr. Mary Bassett was able to do just that.

Before her storied career as New York City Health Commissioner and Harvard professor, Dr. Bassett developed an interest in health care after being a census taker in high school.[61] According to Bassett, she wanted to do more than just "register statistics;" she wanted the opportunity to change lives.

Upon reaching college, Dr. Bassett, who was raised by parents actively involved in the civil rights movement, volunteered at the Black Panther Free Health Center in Roxbury, Massachusetts. Roxbury is a neighborhood with predominantly low-income, Black patients. Bassett realized the patients coming to the free clinic were not intentionally making "poor health choices"; the environment and circumstances around them were causing suffering from various chronic conditions.

As the only Black woman in her graduating class at Columbia's medical school, Bassett pushed through racial bias in classroom settings, going on to become a medical resident at Harlem Hospital. Bassett's medical residency occurred during the time of uncertainty—not unlike the COVID-19 crisis that stopped the globe in its tracks in early 2020—with

---

61   Peter Wortsman, "Alumni Profile: Mary T. Bassett '79 -- A Champion of Health Equity at the Helm of the NYC Department of Health," *Columbia Medicine*, accessed on April 15, 2020.

the confluence of the HIV/AIDS and crack epidemics. Challenges with identifying how to combat HIV/AIDS abounded, along with Bassett's understanding that clinical treatment wasn't enough to keep her patients healthy.

Shortly after her residency, a young, bright-eyed Bassett set off to Zimbabwe, a new, burgeoning African country that had just survived civil war, to help establish a public health system and teach at the University of Zimbabwe. What was expected to be a one to two-year stint became seventeen years. During that time, Bassett learned a lot from her young colleagues at Zimbabwe's ministry of health. They were committed to ensuring expanded access to medical care, especially for rural populations.

Within ten years of achieving independence, the percentage of children who were fully immunized climbed from 25 percent to 80 percent.[62] Five years after achieving independence, Zimbabwe recorded its first HIV/AIDS case. This quickly became a death sentence to all those diagnosed. Over the years, Bassett had to look friends, colleagues, and community members in the eye to tell them that they were diagnosed with a disease for which, at the time, there would be no recovery.

Bassett pushed onward. She led workshops in schools and clinics aimed at encouraging people to change their sexual behaviors. She led research efforts. But she didn't consider thinking about structural change. Structural change was

---

62   Bassett, Mary. "Why your doctor should care about social justice." Filmed November 2015 in New York, NY. TED video, 13:42.

what was in the way of successfully combatting the HIV/ AIDS crisis globally, but also in the United States.

Most clinicians and public health professionals, according to Bassett, feel most comfortable when using their technical skills to try to stop the spread of disease. However, in order to keep people healthy, social structures need to be more closely examined. In Zimbabwe, mostly poor, rural, Black people were suffering from the disease, while whites were relatively unscathed, recreating colonialist history.

Bassett has been candid about feeling she could have done more to speak out against the injustices of the HIV/AIDS crisis at the time. Her experience in Zimbabwe fueled her understanding that while medical professionals overwhelmingly rely on their ability to provide technical expertise, they are often silent in the face of structural violence. Structural violence, according to medical anthropologist Paul Farmer, occurs because "inequities are embedded in the political and economic organization of our social world, often in ways that are invisible to those with privilege and power; and violence because its impact—premature deaths, suffering, illness—is violent."[63]

Her time in Zimbabwe greatly affected the way Bassett approached public health upon returning to the United States. Recognizing that people's environments determine their health choices, she became committed to promoting positive, healthy behaviors. After becoming appointed as NYC Health Commission's Health Promotion and Disease

---

63   Ibid.

Prevention Director, she continued to push for such policies, such as adding calorie postings for dishes offered at fast food restaurants and leading the charge on banning sugary drinks.

In 2014, Bassett was offered the position of NYC Health Commissioner, making her in charge of the health outcomes of over 8 million people. Keeping structural violence in mind, Bassett created the Center for Health Equity in the New York Department of Health and Mental Hygiene.[64] By identifying health inequities, measuring them, and spreading the message, the Center is dedicated to naming the problem of racism both individually and institutionally.

The center supports the efforts of the Department of Health and Mental Hygiene by supporting internal reforms, building partnerships with outside organizations and city agencies, making injustice visible through data and storytelling, and, most importantly, investing in historically underserved communities that have suffered from discriminatory policies. Some of the center's success stories include working with local officials and the Department of Transportation to put bike lanes in Brownsville, Brooklyn—a historically underserved neighborhood.

In the South Bronx, which leads New York City in terms of negative health disparities, the Center partnered with corner stores and bodegas to ensure healthy offerings. In Bassett's words, these strategies are essential to improving

64 NYC Department of Health and Mental Hygiene, "NYC Department of Health and Mental Hygiene - Center for Health Equity," YouTube video, October 30, 2015.

the health of those communities. Most importantly, these neighborhoods shouldn't be viewed as "needy"; there needs to be an understanding that they were rendered unhealthy because of lack of access to fair wages and affordable housing.

Other achievements that Bassett obtained in her four-year tenure as commissioner have included writing prolifically about the impact of gentrification on the health of historically marginalized communities and contributing to a statewide blueprint to end the spread of AIDS.[65]

During her tenure as NYC Health Commissioner, the #BlackLivesMatter movement was gaining national traction.[66] After the murder of Trayvon Martin, an unarmed Black teenager, at the hands of George Zimmerman, the nation was watching to see justice delivered for Martin's family. When Zimmerman was acquitted, activists Patrisse Khan-Cullors, Alicia Garza, and Opal Tometi were spurred to bring attention to the structural violence members of the Black community face when interacting with the police. Medical students didn't stay silent either. With photos of medical students participating in die-ins, a form of protest in which participants simulate being dead, it was clear younger members of the medical professional community wanted to take action.

---

65 Meico Whitlock, "NYC Health Commissioner Dr. Mary Bassett Receives Nicholas A. Rango Leadership Award for More Than 30 Years of Leadership in Addressing HIV-Related Inequalities," *NASTAD,* May 25, 2016.

66 Black Lives Matter, "6 Years Later and Black Activists are Still Fighting: An Open Letter from Black Lives Matter Global Network Co-Founder and Strategic Advisor Patrisse Khan-Cullors," accessed on April 14, 2020.

Medical students also began establishing organizations such as White Coats 4 Black Lives, striving for equity in their educational experience and beyond.[67] In recognition, Bassett penned an often-cited article in the *New England Journal of Medicine* titled "#BlackLivesMatter—A Challenge to the Medical and Public Health Communities."[68]

In it, she writes, "If we fail to explicitly examine our policies and fail to engage our staff in discussions of racism and health, especially at this time of public dialogue about race relations, we may unintentionally bolster the status quo even as society is calling for reform." By expressing this view, Bassett makes clear that if you are not actively fighting structural violence, you may be inadvertently supporting it. In her piece, she was able to bring life into some of the regularly cited health care disparities statistics:

- In 2017, 12.6 percent of Black children had asthma, compared with 7.7 percent of non-Hispanic white children.
- 42 percent of Black adults over age twenty suffer from hypertension, compared with 28.7 percent of non-Hispanic white adults.
- There are 11 infant deaths per 1,000 live births among Black Americans; this is almost twice the national average of 5.8 infant deaths per 1,000 live births.

Bassett hasn't stopped supporting these otherwise radical notions of integrating justice into her work as a clinical

67   White Coats for Black Lives, "Our Mission," accessed on April 15, 2020.
68   Mary Bassett, "#BlackLivesMatter: A Challenge to the Medical and Public Health Communities," *New England Journal of Medicine* 372 (2015); 1085-1087.

practitioner. Nowadays, you can probably find Bassett grabbing a cup of coffee near Harvard Square before heading to her office at The François-Xavier Bagnoud Center for Health and Human Rights at Harvard University.[69]

No matter where she's been—as a teenager recording statistics in someone's home in 1970s New York City, a young physician and professor in the 1980s in Harare, or a fierce advocate for racial justice as New York City Health Commissioner—Bassett's words are clear: lack of action is tantamount to no action. Integrating justice into clinical and administrative health practice is the key to moving things forward.

**

The ability of Black people to live healthy, dignified lives was stripped away from them at the very start. With so many Black Americans having arrived to this country's shores in chains, to then being utilized in medical experiments, to then being treated at subpar, low quality health care facilities, the legacy of pain and oppression lives on in how Black people access health care.

This legacy carries on beyond health care—it has not allowed Black communities to live in high-quality, affordable housing; for Black children to access high-quality education; or for Black people to access better economic opportunities that

---

69 FXB Center for Health and Human Rights at Harvard University, "Mary T. Bassett MD, MPH," accessed on April 17, 2020.

allow them to live lives of dignity. This legacy lives on among Black immigrants from Africa and the Caribbean—among other places—as their children grow up in America and become coded as Black. Their health outcomes deteriorate over time because of increased exposure to racist systems, especially that of health care.

In this history comprised largely of pain, trauma, and deception, there have been a few rising hopes. W. E. B. DuBois is celebrated as a critical thinker and Black intellectual who brought to the fore how the "Negro problem" originated from a predominantly white society imposing restrictions and limiting access to opportunity.

Providers like Dr. W. Montague Cobb and Dr. George Simkins led the fight to ensure America's hospitals were desegregated, using political pressure and legislation to spearhead a movement that would allow Black and white people to access care from the same places.

Dr. Mary Bassett has committed to integrating politics and human rights in her clinical practice and public health policy, allowing #BlackLivesMatter to take center stage.

With the death of George Floyd at the hands of the Minneapolis Police Department in May 2020, the marginalization of Black life has become even more apparent. Protest marches erupted across the country, in cities and towns large and small, in a way that felt like it was fully reckoning with racial injustice.

Political movements evolve over time. Current movements were built on the shoulders of the giants leading the civil rights movement of the 1960s.

And health care touches every part of it.

PART TWO

THOSE WHO CAME LATER

CHAPTER 3

NOT JUST A MODEL MINORITY: ASIAN AMERICANS AND ACCESS TO HEALTH CARE

"I don't think people understand the model-minority stereotype is negative. You are boxed in. You have to untangle that to find your own path."

—AUTHOR, CHEF, AND RESTAURATEUR EDDIE HUANG

Asia is a massive continent, spanning thousands of miles. With multiple religions practiced and hundreds of languages spoken there, it is one of the most diverse continents on the planet. Even within Asia, subregional categories serve as identity markers—East Asian (comprising China, Japan, and South Korea), South Asian (made of India, Pakistan,

Nepal, Bangladesh, Myanmar, Sri Lanka, and Afghanistan), and Southeast Asia (comprising the Philippines, Malaysia, Cambodia, Vietnam, Singapore, Laos, Indonesia, among others). Other groups often grouped as "Asian" include Pacific Islanders (including those from Guam, the American Samoa, Micronesia, and Polynesian islands), Native Hawaiians, Indo-Caribbeans, and Arab Americans.

However, when someone is called "Asian American," many assumptions are made. The term itself seems a misnomer, diluting the incredible diversity of those who come to the United States from a continent consisting of more than 60 percent of the world's population.[70] Even within the United States, Asian American histories are different depending on countries of origin.

***

The Chinese were the only racial group to be explicitly excluded by legislation. The Chinese Exclusion Act, passed by Congress in 1882, was a response to Chinese workers coming to the United States to work on railroads and open up small businesses.[71] The passage of the Chinese Exclusion Act was enabled by those fanning the flames of claims the Chinese were bringing disease, filth, and sexual depravity to American shores.[72]

---

70   UNFPA Asia and the Pacific, "What we do: Population trends," accessed on March 30, 2020.
71   The National Archives Our Documents, "Chinese Exclusion Act (1882)," accessed on March 30, 2020.
72   Kat Chow, "As Chinese Exclusion Act Turns 135, Experts Point to Parallels Today," NPR, May 5, 2017.

Their counterparts to the east, Japanese Americans—many of whom were US citizens born and raised in America—were infamously interned in camps in response to the Japanese attack on Pearl Harbor, relegating them to the rank of second-class citizens.[73] Indian citizens came to the United States in the early 1900s in search of manual work on the railroads alongside their Chinese counterparts but were routinely rioted against by white workers.[74]

On the US Census and most government applications, Pacific Islanders from US territories like Guam and the American Samoa as well as Native Hawaiians are often grouped with Asians, despite having incredibly different origin stories.

Hawaii was originally a thriving kingdom taken by force by the United States government once it was determined how lucrative fruit and sugar sales would be if the United States did not have to pay import taxes.[75] After becoming the fiftieth state, Native Hawaiian people were routinely ignored and undermined because of the federal government's need to ensure assimilation with the mainland.

Guam's native Chamorro people have been routinely persecuted and colonized first by the Spanish, and then by the United States. Historically aggressive tobacco advertising and general neglect from the federal government have resulted

---

73 The National Archives, "Japanese-American Internment During World War II," March 17, 2020.

74 Ananya Bhattacharya, "Indian immigrants have it bad in Donald Trump's America. But the early 1900s were worse," *Quartz*, July 16, 2019.

75 History.com, "Americans overthrow Hawaiian monarchy," February 9, 2010.

in lower quality of life for Guam residents.[76] Moreover, after World War II, destruction of farmland and increased opportunity to make money resulted in increased reliance on US imports and therefore increased obesity and diabetes among the population in Guam.[77]

Another group with a lesser known history in the Asian American community are the Indo-Caribbeans.[78] Indo-Caribbeans are from Caribbean nations with East Indian ancestry. The first Indo-Caribbeans were brought from Calcutta—in the Indian state of Bengal in east India—to Guyana as indentured servants. The British Empire officially abolished slavery in 1838, and so it needed these indentured servants to work the land in the Caribbean. A high percentage of the Indians coming over were from the lowest rungs of the Indian social system. More importantly, these Indians were "recruited" to work in the Caribbean by way of kidnapping or forced detention.

Women in particular were subject to sexual violence and coercion, finding their way to the Caribbean without support or help. Moreover, Indians had a difficult experience settling in the Caribbean, facing backlash from the local Caribbean communities as well as their British masters. Many decades removed from Indians first touching upon

---

76 U.S. Department of Health and Human Services, Office of Minority Health, *Health Disparities Among Pacific Islanders*, by Neal A. Palafox and Momi Kaanoi, Open-file one-pager 2000.

77 Tamar Celis, "From farmer to forager: WWII CHamorus survive on family ranch, starve in concentration camp, " *Pacific Daily News,* January 13, 2019.

78 Elizabeth Jaikaran, "The Indo-Caribbean Experience: Now and Then," *Huffington Post,* December 6, 2017.

the shores of countries like Guyana, Trinidad and Tobago, Jamaica, etc., hundreds of Indo-Caribbeans migrated to the United States in the face of political upheaval in Caribbean countries.[79]

***

While the first Asian immigrants to the United States were often lower-income and less skilled, more highly skilled, well-educated Asians started moving to the United States subsequently. This was, in part, due to the Immigration and Nationality Act of 1965.[80] This law was more interested in attracting immigrants to the United States to unite them with family members who were current citizens. The law was also interested in making Asian immigrants legal permanent residents because of their technical skills and professional qualifications.

This greatly differed from earlier immigration policies that were rooted in admitting (and not admitting) people of certain races and ethnicities. Given that a vast majority of immigrants who settled in the United States at this time were originally from Europe, the only way for Asians to gain a foothold was to have professional qualifications. While some Asians could come to America through family ties, this was much more unlikely given how few Asians were already in

---

79 Joseph Berger, "Indian, Twice Removed," *The New York Times,* December 17, 2004.

80 Muzaffar Chishti, Faye Hipsman, and Isabel Ball, "Fifty Years On, the 1965 Immigration Nationality Act Continues to Reshape the United States," Migration Policy Institute, October 15, 2015.

America. This ensured that a huge cohort of Asian professionals—lawyers, doctors, bankers, teachers, etc.—came to the United States with their families.

President Lyndon B. Johnson signing the Immigration Act of 1965 in New York City, with members of his Cabinet looking on. This piece of legislation allowed highly educated workers from Asia—and those with family ties in the United States—to migrate to the United States.
Source: Wikimedia Commons[81]

Not all Asian immigrants were highly skilled workers and highly educated, however. As mentioned above, much of Asian immigration is also rooted in US intervention in different countries in Asia. The United States, for a time, had colonized the Philippines, a country previously colonized by the Spanish, resulting in large numbers of Filipino families

81   Yoichi Okamoto, "President Lyndon B. Johnson signs the bill into law as Vice President Hubert Humphrey, Senators Edward M. Kennedy and Robert F. Kennedy and others look on," Wikipedia images, October 3, 1965.

moving to America. Still other Asian Americans came from war-torn countries as refugees, such as survivors of Cambodia's Pol Pot regime and those who fled because of violence during the Vietnam War.

***

As the Asian population in the United States began to balloon across the rest of the century, assumptions began to be made about these communities. Asian Americans quickly became termed as the "model minority," known for their hardworking ethic, high educational and income attainment, and major contributions to the American economy and society.[82]

While the "model minority" myth touts positive images of the Asian American community, it does not account for the "bamboo ceiling" that highly educated Asian Americans face in terms of job promotion.[83] It also does not address how some highly qualified Asian Americans may be unable to achieve their potential because of language barriers and lack of degree equivalency (or degree qualifications for high-skilled jobs).

Unfortunately, the model minority myth has also exacerbated stereotypes of Asian Americans being quiet and docile, doing whatever is necessary to assimilate in

---

82 Kat Chow, "'Model Minority' Myth Again Used As A Racial Wedge Between Asians and Blacks," *NPR*, April 19, 2017.

83 Liza Mundy, "Cracking the Bamboo Ceiling: Can Asian American men learn from *Lean In*?" *The Atlantic*, November 2014.

American society. It has also strategically been used as a tool to divide Asian people from other people of color, who were often told that they were not "hardworking enough." In the minds of many, if Asian Americans could make it, why couldn't immigrants from Latin America or Black people?

Moreover, the term does a disservice to Asian Americans who are struggling with real issues of poverty and disenfranchisement. New York City is a great city to profile here, given its incredible Asian American diversity. In New York City in 2017, for example, Asian Americans represented 17.9 percent of New Yorkers living in poverty and had the highest poverty rate of any racial or ethnic group in the city.[84] Moreover, the 2017, data uncovered large disparities within the Asian American community in terms of wealth and earnings: 39.4 percent of Burmese Americans lived in poverty, compared to 6.8 percent of Filipinos.[85] Severe data underreporting, stereotypes that suggest that Asian Americans do not need public assistance programs, and lack of cultural understanding continue to make Asian Americans living in poverty invisible.

---

84 Victoria Tran, "Asian Americans are falling through the cracks in data representation and social services," *Urban Wire* (blog), *The Urban Institute,* June 19, 2018.

85 Ibid.

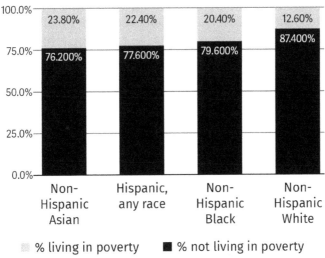

Poverty Rates by Race in NYC (2017)

Comparing poverty rates by race in NYC in 2017.
Source: NYC Mayor's Office for Economic Opportunity[86]

***

So, what does all of this have to do with Asian American health outcomes?

Given the population is so diverse in culture, language, and ethnicity, aggregating all populations can sometimes mask the health risks among different communities. In a paper published by *BMC Public Health*, Gordon and colleagues studied the prevalence of health conditions among

---

86   NYC Mayor's Office for Economic Opportunity, "Poverty Data: Data Tool."

Asian patients in northern California.[87] It was found that diabetes prevalence among South Asians, Filipinos, and Pacific Islanders was higher compared to any other racial group surveyed. Hypertension prevalence for all Asians was worse than white people but better than Black people, with Filipinos and Pacific Islanders suffering from the highest rates of hypertension among Asian community members.

Health inequities research on Asian Americans, typically touted as being healthier than their white counterparts, is fairly new. Until now, much research on Asian Americans and Pacific Islanders have been focused on social class, identity politics, and professional and political success.[88] Similar to Gordon et al.'s paper, Adia and colleagues found stark health disparities when data was disaggregated by Asian country of origin.[89] Japanese Americans tended to have higher rates of obesity compared to their non-Latine white and Asian peers, while Filipino Americans had greater prevalence of high blood pressure, diabetes, and heart disease compared to their Asian counterparts.

87　Nancy P. Gordon et al., "Aggregation of Asian-American subgroups mask meaningful differences in health and health risks among Asian ethnicities: an electronic health record based cohort study," *BMC Public Health* 19, (2019): 1 - 14.

88　Constante, Agnes, "New study reveals previously invisible health issues among Asians in U.S.," *NBC News*, February 24, 2020.

89　Alexander C. Adia, Jennifer Nazareno, Don Operario, and Ninez A. Ponce, "Health Conditions, Outcomes, and Service Access Among Filipino, Vietnamese, Chinese, Japanese, and Korean Adults in California, 2011-2017," *American Journal of Public Health* 110, no. 4 (2020): 520-526.

Other markers have also emerged in research. To learn more, I spoke with health researcher Dr. Stella Yi from New York University's Center for the Study of Asian American Health. Dr. Yi, who is trained as a cardiovascular epidemiologist, focuses a lot of her research on nutrition and health outcomes in the Asian American community. In particular, she is interested in the impact of physical activity on Asian American lifestyle and health.

Speaking over Zoom, she shared it has been established in the literature that "South Asians are at a particularly high risk of cardiovascular disease, Filipinos are at a really high risk for obesity, Chinese Americans have elevated hemoglobin A1-C [making them high-risk for type 2 diabetes], and Pacific Islanders have really high rates of smoking."

However, according to Dr. Yi, we need to be mindful when we talk about disaggregating data about Asian Americans by country of origin. Firstly, we do not always see Asian Americans represented in health care access research and disparity data. In a study from the *American Journal of Public Health* documenting Obamacare's impact on insurance rates across ethnic groups, the analysis did not include Asian Americans. Since Asian Americans have not "historically" been documented as having health access challenges, they were not included in the survey or study design.

Highlighting that a lot of data about Asian Americans is already thinly documented, Dr. Yi recognizes that existing data about Asian Americans, if it exists, is aggregated across country of origin and ethnic groups. According to Dr. Yi, it is necessary to assess data from national sources alongside locally collected sources that are considered "culturally appropriate" or even conducted a bit differently.

In an interview, she mentioned, "It's very challenging to provide meaningful disaggregated data collection from a participant burden perspective. If you want to say that you're meaningfully reaching all of these populations, you need linguistic translations to be representative of lower income communities."

As an example, she mentioned how data is collected by the National Health Interview Survey.

"Let's say that the National Health Interview survey puts out a call for people to, you know, they're doing random digit dialing for people to respond to a health survey, and they're only conducting it in English and Spanish. The people they're going to reach are going to be heavily skewed toward the higher end of the income distribution."

As a result, Asian Americans across the board appear healthier—and wealthier—in aggregated data. To that end, the model minority myth plagues Asian Americans negatively in the context of health as well. Beyond not receiving as much money from social services allotted by New York City government, Dr. Yi has reported instances of people trying to explain away disparities.

For example, after presenting results on a comparative study that found that Asian Americans had the lowest levels of physical activity compared to other racial groups in New York City and Los Angeles, a response Dr. Yi got was "You didn't mention tai chi in your question. What about all those seniors in Chinatown doing exercises in the park?"

Additional barriers to care for Asian Americans go beyond just linguistic challenges. Asian Americans have pretty high insurance coverage rates, whether through private insurance or through Medicaid. However, beyond language access, there are challenges with understanding the health care system itself and how to navigate it.

"It's this whole level of [health] literacy that immigrants face and it's not exclusive to Asian Americans. It applies to other groups like Hispanics too. [For these groups], community-based organizations become these warehouses where people go, and they need help with navigating step-by-step processes of getting access to care."

These community-based organizations tend to do some of the work of cultural translation and navigation for Asian Americans. While Asian American organizations are not as numerous because of the relatively short history of Asian migration and smaller population sizes, NYU continues to work and partner with them to identify community-oriented interventions to improve health in their local communities.

**

Intergenerational trauma also plays a role among certain Asian American community members. Asian Americans and Pacific Islanders who have experienced violence, war, and oppression prior to arriving in the United States suffer more frequent psychological distress.[90] Moreover, talking about mental health in these communities is considered highly taboo. Mental health in Asian American communities can be further exacerbated by being bombarded with messages of assimilation, making it challenging to hold onto the culture of their countries of origin.

There have been increasing efforts to recognize the unique challenges Asian Americans and Pacific Islanders face. Bigger strides have been made to improve care for this population as awareness about the need for culturally competent care has increased. According to University of Chicago health ethics professor Dr. Marshall Chin, "The Association of Asian Pacific Community Health Organizations (AAP-CHO), the National Association of Community Health Centers (NACHC), and the Oregon Primary Care Association (OPCA) have created the Protocol for Responding to and Assessing Patient Assets, Risks, and Experiences (PRAPARE) tool to screen for needs such as housing, employment, transportation, safety, and social support."[91]

Dr. Marshall Chin has been at the forefront of health equity and health disparities mitigation for several years. With a background in ethics and internal medicine, Dr. Chin has participated in studies to improve diabetes and outcomes in

---

90   Gayle Y. Imawasa, "Recommendations for the Treatment of Asian-American/Pacific Islander Populations," *Psychological Treatment of Ethnic Minority Populations: Asian American Psychological Association.*

91   Marshall H. Chin, "Addressing Social Needs and Structural Inequities to Reduce Health Disparities: A Call to Action for Asian American Heritage Month," *National Minority Health Month Blog* (blog), *Office of Minority Health,* May 15, 2019.

federally qualified health centers (FQHCs) serving vulnerable populations, including Asian Americans.

In recent years, there has been an increasing focus on eliminating language barriers. While many providers are committed to treating a wide variety of patients, being able to speak with them in their language of choice is challenging, especially given Asia's diversity as a continent. In some cases, this results in Asian immigrants' children becoming the cultural brokers for their family members' health care.

In Vikki Katz's paper "Children as Brokers of Their Immigrant Families' Health-Care Connections," she finds that "children broker to compensate for the limited (or nonexistent) accommodations institutions make for diverse populations."[92] While adult interpreters are able to translate strictly for medical purposes, the presence of family members who are fluent in English ensure cultural translation of what is occurring during the doctor's visit as well. As such, Asian Americans typically enlist the help, support, and decision-making of family members when considering health-related choices.

When considering improving access for this population, it is necessary to recognize the value and role of family members in helping Asian Americans—particularly those who are older and are not fluent in English—in obtaining care. Empowering family members to explain and support patient decisions is critical to making an unfamiliar health care

---

92   Vikki Katz, "Children as Brokers of Their Immigrant Families' Health-Care Connections," *Social Problems* 61, no. 2: 194 - 215.

system more palatable and easier to navigate. Family members—in concert with community-based organizations who cater to Asian Americans—can support access to care for parents, guardians, aunts, uncles, and other Asian American community members.

**

The history of how people arrive in the United States—and in what capacities they are allowed to enter—has consequences for future generations. While the first Asians to arrive in the United States were railroad workers and daily wage earners, the racism and xenophobia undergirding immigration policies caused very little Asian emigration to the United States.

It is critical to remember the discrimination faced by Asians and Pacific Islanders once they arrived to or became included in the United States. East Asians were referred to as the "yellow peril," South Asians faced discrimination, and Native Hawaiians, the Chamorro in Guam, and Samoans in American Samoa were and are routinely relegated to second class citizenship.

In an attempt to paint itself as a racial democracy, according to author Ellen Wu, the United States began to take a more favorable view of Asian Americans, painting them as model citizens.[93] As this "model minority myth" has evolved, it has obscured the struggles of lower-income Asians and Pacific

---

93 Jeff Guo, "The real reasons the U.S. became less racist toward Asian Americans," *The Washington Post,* November 26, 2019.

Islanders who are challenged with chronic health conditions and the inability to successfully navigate the American health care system. The model minority myth has also enabled lack of support for Asians who are in need of social services, particularly in urban areas.

Studying health inequity among Asian Americans is finally on the rise. Through the work of people like Dr. Stella Yi, Dr. Marshall Chin, and organizations like NYU's Center for the Study of Asian American Health and the University of Chicago's Center for Asian Health Equity, Asian health inequities are starting to become more visible. Through the right policy and technological interventions, not only will these inequities be made visible; there will also be a path to mitigating them.

CHAPTER 4

SOLIDARIDAD: THE LATINE COMMUNITY'S HEALTH OUTCOMES

"Write what should not be forgotten."

—AUTHOR ISABELLE ALLENDE

Explanatory Note: In the past, people emigrating from Latin America to the United States (and their descendants) were called "Hispanics" or "Latinos." The term "Hispanic" is still used in official government documents, including the 2020 Census. To be more gender inclusive, the term "Latine" has been adopted when referring to those from Latin America. There has been some criticism that the term "Latinx" does not respect existing Spanish grammar rules and has been imposed by non-Spanish speakers. Many younger Americans with roots in Latin America have started referring to themselves as "Latine," to be gender inclusive and also adhere to existing Spanish grammar rules. For the purposes of this section, I will be referring to this community as "Latine."

West Side Story. Evita. In the Heights.

While these colorful Broadway musicals allow a small glimpse into life in a Latine community, there is so much more to examine beyond the synchronized dance moves and casual phrases of Spanglish that we see on stage or on screen. The history of Latin America is rife with the violence of Spanish conquistadors plundering Indigenous communities, colonizing communities, and establishing class structures that ensured light-skinned Spanish people could consolidate their power and that descendants of Indigenous communities were not afforded the same access.

As early as the early twentieth century, the US federal government made clear it had dominion over the Americas, especially when it came to being owed money from their Latin American peers. Taking on the role of regional policeman, President Teddy Roosevelt passed the Roosevelt Corollary, stating the United States would "intervene as a last resort" to ensure Latin American nations would pay their debts.[94] This served as justification for US intervention in Cuba, Nicaragua, Haiti, and the Dominican Republic, among other countries.

These interventions grew in intensity during the Cold War, when the United States and the Soviet Union were jockeying for power among developing nations around the world—including in Latin America. Taking on Puerto Rico as an additional territory while imposing English language

---

94   U.S. Department of State, Office of the Historian. *Roosevelt Corollary to the Monroe Doctrine, 1904,* Washington DC.

rules was another example of the United States asserting its dominance in Spanish-speaking areas. Now, political instability and economic uncertainty have become a mainstay in certain Latin American countries because of the handling of the "war on drugs." According to *The Guardian*, "US-funded aerial fumigation programs and anti-narcotics policing in the southern Andes... only succeeded in pushing the problem north," explaining political violence in Colombia.[95]

Latin America has an inextricable link to the United States because of repeated interventions in governments and elections. These interventions have resulted in an increasing number of people living in Latin America opting to move to the United States for access to better opportunities. Immigration continues to be a key policy issue in this community. According to Pew Research, in 2017, more than half of America's 10.5 million undocumented immigrants came from Mexico and Central America.[96] In 2019, Pew Research also showed that, among all immigrants more broadly, Mexico emerged as the second biggest country of origin sending immigrants to the United States.[97]

95 David Huey, "The US war on drugs and its legacy in Latin America," *The Guardian*, February 3, 2014.

96 Elaine Karmack and Christine Stenglein, "How many undocumented immigrants are in the United States and who are they?" *Voter Vitals* (blog). *Brookings Institute*, November 12, 2019.

97 Jynnah Radford, "Key findings about U.S. immigrants," *Pew Research Center*, June 17, 2019.

Origins of Undocumented Population (2017)

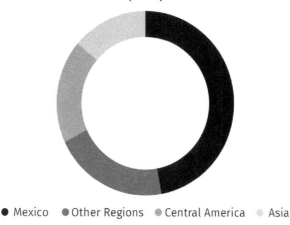

● Mexico ● Other Regions ● Central America ● Asia

Source: Pew Research[98]

***

Certain policies targeting immigrants and their families— which may comprise of some US citizens—have made health care access incredibly difficult.

For example, the recently passed public charge rule states that immigrants applying for lawful permanent resident status—also known as obtaining a Green Card—may have their applications rendered "inadmissible" if they are deemed to have used public services.[99] Public services include Medicaid,

---

98 Elaine Karmack and Christine Stenglein, "How many undocumented immigrants are in the United States and who are they?" *Voter Vitals* (blog). *Brookings Institute,* November 12, 2019.

99 U.S. Citizenship and Immigration Services. *Public Charge Fact Sheet,* Washington DC.

which many low-income families rely on to access medical care.

This is especially damning for immigrant families who use Medicaid's Children's Health Insurance Program to get medical care for their children. As a result, few immigrants are signing up for Medicaid, resulting in an increase in the uninsured population. The Kaiser Family Foundation reported that nearly half of survey-participating community health clinics had immigrant patients who declined to enroll in Medicaid in 2019.[100]

Moreover, undocumented immigrants in particular have no way to access any form of health insurance. Working in industries such as agriculture and fast food, undocumented immigrants are not likely to obtain health insurance through employment and are not eligible to purchase health insurance through any state or federal marketplace.

Lack of economic opportunity for undocumented immigrants also affects where they can afford to live, which may contribute to the development of chronic conditions and stress. Most importantly, the fear of deportation or family separation looms for many undocumented immigrants, who may have children who are citizens or have received special protection through Deferred Action for Childhood Arrival (DACA).

---

100 Jennifer Tolbert, Samantha Artiga, and Olivia Pham, "Impact of Shifting Immigration Policy on Medicaid Enrollment and Utilization of Care among Health Center Patients," *Kaiser Family Foundation*, October 15, 2019.

***

Undocumented immigrants have a unique experience in the United States accessing health care. To learn more, I spoke with twenty-five-year-old Diana Martinez (pseudonym), a student affairs professional and recipient of the Deferred Action for Childhood Arrivals (DACA) program initiated by the Obama administration.[101] If you came to the United States without documentation before you were sixteen years old and arrived before 2012, you were eligible to apply for DACA, provided you had not been convicted of a felony and were currently in some form of schooling. DACA recipients are protected from deportation and are given work permits, which allow them legal status to work.

Martinez was born in El Salvador and came to California at age nine. She was due to graduate from high school in 2013, and so she recognizes she benefited from being at the right age when DACA was announced in 2012.

When asked about her other family members, she mentioned the various immigration statuses in her household. She said, "Some of them have work permits. Some of them don't. A lot of us are still undocumented. And some of us just became residents through partners and having children." This speaks to the experience of undocumented immigrants living in mixed-status families—with some family members who are citizens, permanent residents, and also undocumented.

---

101   University of California Berkeley, "DACA Information," June 23, 2020.

Martinez also spoke of how California state policies supported her ability to afford higher education. While states cannot legalize the status of undocumented immigrants, per the American Immigration Council, they are able to alleviate the issues that come from being undocumented. At least nineteen states, including California, have passed laws that allow undocumented immigrants to receive in-state tuition for public universities. Because of this policy, Martinez said, she was able to apply for financial aid, go to college, and graduate debt free.

However, when it came to health care, Martinez had a different story to share. In an interview, she shared, "Prior to DACA, I didn't access health care. I didn't have any health insurance. In college, I went to the health services on campus that we had. Now that I have a full-time job, I have health insurance."

Martinez's story is not unique to undocumented immigrants. When asked about how she would have paid for emergency care prior to DACA, she mentioned, "I was just kind of floating around, and if there were any emergencies, I would just have to take care of myself one way or another, or have to pay out of pocket." While Martinez never had to receive emergent care, she talked about not receiving preventive care while growing up. In her words, "I kind of just took that risk and didn't have access to everything. I just went through life."

In undergraduate and graduate school, because of her ability to access health care, Martinez was able to take better care of herself. She mentioned accessing mental health services in graduate school through campus health services and being able to get women's health visits and flu shots.

Since the Affordable Care Act, however, Martinez has noticed shifts in insurance status among her family members. While benefits are still limited, it has helped them access preventive services without having to pay all costs out of pocket.

Martinez also highlighted how helpful hospitals and insurance agencies can be in helping undocumented immigrants apply for health insurance. "I know that hospitals do a really good job in talking to parents, families, and other folks who don't have status. They're able to help them apply even if they don't have a Social Security number. A lot of times they can use an ITIN [Individual Tax Identification Number] as a form of identification."

While Martinez's family has been able to access health insurance, this is partially due to being protected by California laws and statutes. Questions around immigration status are under federal purview, but laws passed supporting undocumented immigrants' access to public goods such as health care and education are up to the states. This has left a patchwork of health access—and outcomes—for undocumented immigrants.

***

Extreme social challenges—drug violence, unemployment, and rampant corruption—continue to motivate those living in Latin America to move to the United States. Latine

Americans are one of the fastest growing ethnic groups in the United States. This population growth underscores this community's increasing spending and political power. In 2015, Latine households earned $902.8 billion before taxes and Medicare/Social Security contributions. Despite these contributions, this community faces challenges in its health care.[102]

What does this mean for health and health outcomes?

Like most other marginalized communities, Latine American quality of life is disproportionately impacted by social determinants of health, including socioeconomic status, employment opportunities, and neighborhood resources. Not having access to proper social support systems can increase chronic stress, resulting in unhealthy behaviors such as poor diet and substance use. Moreover, Latine Americans are more likely to be younger, less educated, living below the poverty line, and facing language barriers compared to their other counterparts.[103]

A paper published in *Public Health Reviews* presents a helpful way to think about Latine American access to health and health outcomes.[104] Clearly outlining the different factors at play, this conceptual framework in the chart below recognizes how health services treat and prevent risk factors to reduce

102 New American Economy, "Power of the Purse: How Hispanics Contribute to the U.S. Economy," December 2017.
103 Eduardo Velasco-Mondragon et al., "Hispanic health in the USA: a scoping review of the literature," *Public Health Reviews* (2016) 37:31.
104 Ibid.

morbidity but also influence social determinants and health inequalities that ultimately negatively impact morbidity.

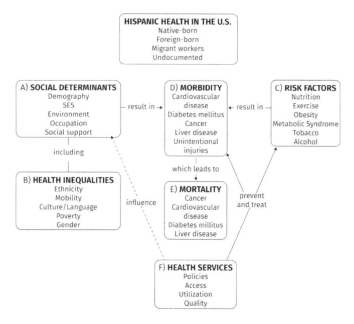

This framework outlines the ways in which Latine people access health care and the relevant challenges they face. Source: *Velasco-Mondragon et al.*[105]

Not only is the health of Latine Americans impacted because of living locations, but where they live also dictates any economic opportunities that may be available to them. Given that health is most influenced by the neighborhood where people live, it is also critical to point out that 91 percent of Latine Americans live in predominantly urban areas, with

---

105 Velasco-Mondragon, E, Jimenez, A, Palladino-Davis, AG, Davis, D, Escamilla-Cejudo, JA. Hispanic health in the USA: a scoping review of the literature. Public Health Reviews, December 7, 2016; 37:31.

about one quarter living near highways. Living near highways exacerbates the likelihood of developing chronic diseases like respiratory illness, cardiovascular diseases, and poor pregnancy outcomes. In general, Latine Americans are more likely to live near areas with high levels of industrial pollution, making general access to clean air and water challenging.

With respect to economic opportunity—which may otherwise allow Latine Americans to move to more affluent neighborhoods—Latine Americans disproportionately perform more low-skilled, high-risk jobs in industries such as construction, domestic maintenance and repair services, and manufacturing. A substantial cohort of Latine Americans also serves as agricultural workers, who predominantly work with their hands and with dangerous farm machinery to pick and harvest crops. Working with such machinery, combined with the long, backbreaking hours in agriculture, Latine Americans who work in the food harvesting business have higher likelihoods of mortality from occupational hazards.[106]

***

One of the earliest people to champion for better working conditions and improved health outcomes for predominantly Latine migrant workers is political activist Dolores Huerta.[107]

---

106 Alma Patty Tzalain, "I Harvest Your Food. Why Isn't My Health 'Essential'?" *The New York Times,* April 15, 2020.

107 The Dolores Huerta Foundation, "Dolores Huerta," Accessed on April 16, 2020.

Outspoken and bold, the petite Huerta was born to parents from Mexico; her father was a union activist who ran for political office in New Mexico's legislature and won, while her mother was an active participant in community affairs and supported low-wage workers. This ethos drove Huerta to go into teaching, but she quickly realized the health issues her students were facing—hunger, malnutrition, and injuries—could only be solved by ensuring their parents, mostly migrant workers, had access to economic rights.

Most known for her phrase *si se puede* (yes we can! in Spanish), Huerta began organizing to allow migrant workers picking grapes access to bathroom breaks, cold drinking water, and rest periods.[108] As political director of the Community Service Organization, she worked with community organizer Fred Ross to raise awareness around the dangerous conditions that farmworkers were toiling in for as low as seventy cents an hour in the 1960s.

In an interview with *NPR*, Huerta also spoke of the health conditions that workers' children were suffering because of poverty: "People were so incredibly poor, and they were working so hard. And the children were [suffering from malnutrition] and very ill-clothed and ill-fed... You saw how hard they were working, and yet they were not getting paid anything."[109] Because of Huerta's active lobbying and campaigning efforts, the Agricultural Labor Relations Act of 1975 was successfully passed, giving farmworkers collective bargaining rights.

---

108 Maria Gody, "Dolores Huerta: The Civil Rights Icon Who Showed Farmworkers 'Si Se Puede'," *NPR,* September 17, 2017.

109 Ibid.

To add fuel to fire, in 2017, pesticides used in Bakersfield, California, were causing workers to experience severe nausea and vomiting. Huerta mentioned these pesticides have caused "so many women [to] have cancer, so many children [to] have been born with deformities." [110]

While Latine Americans have higher likelihoods of developing chronic conditions and injuries endemic to the living and economic opportunities they have been able to access, being able to pay for care is a whole different story.

***

Along with associated health risks brought on by occupational hazards and lifestyles, Latine Americans also have to figure out how to pay for the health care they need. Having health insurance in any form in the United States is a marker of access to health care services. Compared to their non-Latine white counterparts, Latine populations in the United States have lower enrollment rates. Even after the passage of the Affordable Care Act—designed with the explicit intention to expand health insurance coverage—26.4 percent of Latine community members were uninsured compared to 10.4 percent of their non-Latine white counterparts.[111]

---

110 Oliver Milman, "Pesticide that Trump's EPA refused to ban blamed for sickening farm workers," *The Guardian*, May 17, 2017.

111 Samantha Artiga, Kendal Orgera, and Anthony Damico, "Changes in Health Coverage by Race and Ethnicity since the ACA, 2010-2018," *Kaiser Family Foundation*, March 5, 2020.

Especially during the COVID-19 pandemic of 2020, Latine populations have been disproportionately affected by the spread of the disease. Given the nature of their professions—most Latines exist as essential workers—and the neighborhoods they tend to live in, Latines are more likely to have chronic conditions that make them susceptible to the viral disease.

Despite being one of the fastest growing populations in the United States, the Latine population does not receive much attention with respect to its quality of life metrics. However, reproductive justice activist and candidate for New York State Assemblywoman Jessica González-Rojas had some thoughts on how to increase Latine representation in public policy and ensure better access to higher quality health care with better outcomes.

***

What's key to supporting marginalized communities, especially communities of color, is to strategically build capacity in the community to organize and advocate for its own needs. The National Latina Institute for Reproductive Health does just that. Focused on improving access to reproductive care, the Latina Institute (as it is commonly called) often recognizes the other challenges that members of the Latine community face. The Latina Institute is rooted in a deep understanding of intersectionality—the term coined by scholar Kimberlé Crenshaw.

Intersectionality recognizes the multitude of identities that a singular person may hold. In the context of Latina female-identifying people, issues surrounding language access, immigration status, and poverty intersect with the ability to receive reproductive care.

Former executive director Jessica González-Rojas joined the Latina Institute in 2004 as a policy director.[112] With an energetic twinkle in her eye, González-Rojas made her life's work come true throughout her time at the institute. With a background in public policy and supporting students of color, González-Rojas recognized the value of having "a political home where Latinidad (Latine solidarity) met reproductive justice, social justice, and LGBTQ+ liberation."

According to González-Rojas, the Latina Institute is grounded in three main actions: policy advocacy, grassroots community organizing, and consciousness-shifting within communities. What is critically important to the institute is that equal work is done to shift both policy and cultural narratives around marginalized communities. By deploying social justice frameworks in otherwise health-related spaces, the Latina Institute is able to build power within the Latine community and advocate for community members in policy circles.

***

Policy Advocacy
Policy advocacy at Latine Institute is focused on representing the voice of Latine community members in certain spaces.[113]

---

112 LinkedIn, "Jessica (Jessica Gonzalez) Gonzalez-Rojas."
113 National Latina Institute for Reproductive Justice, "Latina Advocacy Networks,"

The Latina Institute was at the table during the development of the Affordable Care Act (ACA), especially the Women's Health Amendment. They fought to include abortion and immigration, and while it didn't happen, the Latina Institute still supported the ACA in its effort to increase insurance coverage.

The ACA is critically important for the Latine community, which is the minority racial community with the largest amount of uninsured people.[114] According to the Kaiser Family Foundation, Latine community members have significantly higher uninsured rates compared to their white counterparts, standing at 19 percent of the Latine population being uninsured.

The Latina Institute was also very active in efforts to repeal the Hyde Amendment, which prevents the use of public dollars in abortion provision.[115] The Latina Institute worked with other women's organizations led by other racial communities (National Asian Pacific American Women's Forum, National Network of Abortion Funds, SisterSong) to push for abortion access for low-income women in these communities.[116]

---

114 Jennifer Tolbert, Kendal Orgera, and Natalie Singer, "Key Facts about the Uninsured Population," *Kaiser Family Foundation*, December 13, 2019.

115 National Latina Institute for Reproductive Health, "Sin Seguro, No Mas! Without Coverage, No More: Latinx's Access to Abortion Under Hyde," Fact Sheet October 2018.

116 National Latina Institute for Reproductive Justice, "Reproductive Justice organizations express dismay that the Hyde amendment was added to the Labor, Health and Human Services, Education, and Related Agencies spending bill," May 8, 2019.

This effort was challenging at times because mainstream reproductive justice organizations were worried about getting access to family planning through Title X. Title X is a federal grant program created in 1970 to fund family planning and preventive health services, though not abortion access.[117] Many mainstream reproductive justice organizations were concerned with the "gag rule," which prevents providers working at Title X-funded institutions from referring patients for abortion care.

However, González-Rojas stressed that often those at the margins of society—namely low-income women of color—suffer most from policies such as Title X's "gag rule" and the Hyde Amendment. According to Gonzalez-Rojas, the Latina Institute has deployed a variety of political strategies—polling, education workshops on college campuses and in local communities, etc.—and were successful in building the Each Woman Act.[118] While the Hyde Amendment is still in place, there has been incredible political momentum to support its repeal, especially among Democrats.

Lastly, outside of specifically reproductive justice contexts, the Latina Institute has been at the table ensuring that Latine community members are heavily involved in conversations about comprehensive immigration reform, public charge rules, changes in welfare/public benefits policy, etc.[119] Latina Institute recognizes women of color are often not included in critical policy conversations. By bringing the concerns of

117 "What is Title X? An Explainer," PRH.
118 Megan K. Donovan, "EACH Woman Act Offers Bold Path Toward Equitable Abortion Coverage," *Guttmacher Institute,* March 2019.
119 National Latina Institute for Reproductive Justice, "What We Do."

these community members to the table, it can inform more comprehensive policymaking.

Community Organizing and Consciousness-Shifting

The Latina Institute also recognizes the power of community organizing and consciousness-shifting. Part of community organizing efforts has included partnering with community health clinics and abortion providers to ensure culturally competent, gender-affirming care is provided. This is critically important in the work that the Latina Institute does in order to support transgender Latine people. By educating providers at conferences and workshops, especially by showcasing stories from real patients, the Latina Institute has been able to build capacity among clinicians to ensure they can best support Latine patients.

Consciousness shifting is a core part of the Latina Institute's work as well. This is especially important given the messaging that young Latine community members receive about themselves—namely, that they are a drain on the system and inherently contribute to the cycle of poverty. Through extensive workshopping and coalition building, the Latina Institute has not only been able to recruit high-potential community members, but it has also used community organizing as a pathway to grow in the ranks of the organization.

The Latina Institute is perfectly situated among a variety of social justice issues such as immigrant rights, reproductive health, and women's empowerment. According to González-Rojas, "We're the group in the women's rights community saying 'What about Latinas? What about immigrants?' and in Latino civil rights spaces saying 'What about women? What about gender?'" By being able to truly represent intersectionality in these different social issues, the Latina Institute is able to advocate successfully on behalf of the Latine community.

***

The Latine community continues to organize around issues of immigration, housing, and health care on a regular basis. As one of the fastest growing populations—and voting blocs—in the United States, they are making their voices heard through demonstrations, protests, lobbying, and other forms of advocacy. Young professionals affected by immigration status, like Diana Martinez, provide context for how status and health access are intrinsically linked.

By leading the fight for dignity, better wages, and improved working conditions, Dolores Huerta made the voice of the farmworker—arguably the most important being at the start of the food production cycle, and, tragically, the most unheard—loud and clear. Political and reproductive justice activists like Jessica González-Rojas continue to be at the forefront of empowering Latine women and gender non-conforming people to own their identities and make the reproductive choices best for them.

A rich history of Latine community organizing and advocacy in this country continues. On behalf of health care, Latine individuals have advocated for improved access to care for undocumented Latine people, for improved language access for those who do not speak English as a first language, and others.

And in the foreground, *"El pueblo unido jamás será vencido"*—a rallying cry used in Chile in the 1970s and used in English-speaking countries as "the people united will never be defeated"—continues to resound.

PART THREE

THOSE WHO WERE FORGOTTEN

CHAPTER 5

THE AMERICAN HEARTLAND: ACCESSING HEALTH CARE IN RURAL AMERICA

———

"You know, rural Americans are a special people. Their labor puts food on our table and fuel in our gas tanks. Their service in our military sets a powerful example of leadership, honor, and sacrifice. Their spirit of community inspires us all."

—TOM VILSACK, FORMER SECRETARY OF AGRICULTURE

The COVID-19 pandemic that ravaged the United States—and the globe—in early 2020 has highlighted and exacerbated already existing challenges in health care access for vulnerable populations. This continues to be true of a population comprised of 46 million Americans but is often forgotten: rural America.[120]

Chronic Disease and Condition Prevalence (2014)

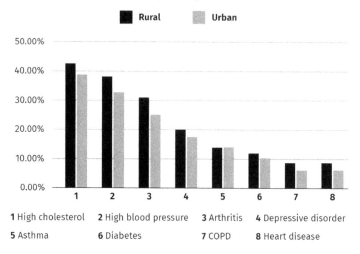

Source: *Centers for Disease Control, Rural Health Information Hub*[121]

While those living in crowded metropolises face their own set of challenges, rural Americans are typically older, sicker, and less likely to be insured or seek preventive services.[122] According to the Centers for Disease Control and Prevention (CDC), rural Americans are more likely to experience preventable death from causes such as heart disease, cancer, unintentional injuries, and stroke.

120 Centers for Disease Control, "Rural Health: About Rural Health."
121 Rural Health Information Hub, "Chronic Diseases and Condition Prevalence."
122 Ibid.

Moreover, hospitals and medical facilities are few and far in between, requiring rural Americans to travel long distances to the emergency room. This has proven especially challenging for rural women who are pregnant or new mothers, resulting in increased maternal and infant mortality rates.

According to a December 2019 *Health Affairs* article, by 2014, more than half of rural counties had no hospitals providing maternity care.[123] While this may not be the best measure to track access to maternity care, it does indicate the challenges that expectant and new mothers might face in being able to proactively prevent pregnancy-related health issues. The study also found that rural mothers had a 9 percent higher likelihood of experiencing some form of maternal morbidity and mortality compared to their urban counterparts.

While some rural expectant mothers may opt to use the services of a traveling midwife, they may run into issues with credentials and payment regardless. A 2019 *New Yorker* article profiled Sunday Smith, a woman who may be the only certified nurse-midwife offering services in a one hundred-mile radius.[124] The article covers her trips to various homes to give birth, revealing the challenges she faces in getting to her patients on time and how she is often paid in agricultural products.

---

123 Katy Backes Kozhimannil, Julia D. Interrante, Carrie Henning-Smith, and Lindsay K. Admon, "Rural-Urban Differences in Severe Maternal Morbidity and Mortality in the US, 2007 - 2015," *Health Affairs* 38, no. 12, December 2019.

124 Emily Bobrow, "A Midwife in the North Country," *The New Yorker*, December 22, 2019.

Another service of critical importance in rural areas is mental health.

While labor and delivery can't be done over the phone, increasing access for rural residents through telehealth does show some promise. However, many areas may not be equipped with broadband to allow that to happen. According to the 2018 Broadband Deployment Report, only 69.3 percent of rural areas and 64.6 percent of tribal areas had access to what the Federal Communications Commission (FCC), a government body, deems high-speed broadband Internet.[125]

Hospitals in rural areas continue to face financial challenges, resulting in extensive hospital closures; in Alabama alone, thirteen hospitals across the state have closed over the past ten years, with seven of them in rural areas.[126] The loss of hospitals in remote areas can have devastating effects on a community member's ability to access preventive and critical services and can result in economic decline.

Of particular importance is the states with the highest number of rural hospital closures—Texas, Tennessee, Georgia, Alabama, Mississippi, and North Carolina—having all chosen not to expand Medicaid. While hospital closure is contingent on several factors, a *Health Affairs* article confirms that "Medicaid expansion was associated with improved hospital

125 Rural Health Information Hub, "Barriers to Telehealth in Rural Areas."
126 Mike Baird and Deanna Larson, "Telehealth's untapped potential in rural America," *Medical Economics,* February 7, 2020.

financial performance and substantially lower likelihoods of closure, especially in rural markets."[127]

In many local economies, hospitals are a significant source of employment; when they close, many lose jobs in the process. According to Dena McDonough, associate director of health policy at Washington, DC-based think tank Bipartisan Policy Center (BPC), the current US health care system is now without a sufficient volume to pay for the high overhead of staffing. Given smaller populations in rural areas, it continues to be increasingly difficult for smaller hospitals to continue staffing when volumes are not helping compensate for overhead costs.

***

As the United States shifts, health care policy seeks to incentivize increased participation in value-based models, and rural hospitals are challenged by this prospect. McDonough shared in an interview:

"There's a huge amount of cost that goes into developing the infrastructure; it's a total change in workflow."

The federal government has already recognized the challenge of providing health care in rural settings. For this reason, certain hospitals in rural areas are designated as critical access hospitals (CAHs) because they provide care

127 Adam Searing, "More Rural Hospitals Closing in States Refusing Medicaid Coverage Expansion," *Rural Health Policy Project*, October 29, 2018.

to patients who would otherwise have limited or no access. Defined as health care facilities with fewer than twenty-five beds, located at least thirty-five miles away from the nearest hospital, providing 24/7 emergency services, and maintaining an average length of stay of ninety-six hours for acute care/inpatient care episodes, CAHs are reimbursed with the understanding that they provide significant care for a very small population.[128]

Outside of these basic challenges, rural populations are vulnerable to other circumstances that can exacerbate health problems. For example, rural residents are more likely to be socially isolated, which increases loneliness. Former Surgeon General Dr. Vivek Murthy has written extensively about loneliness as an increasing public health concern in the United States.

According to Dr. Murthy, those who struggle with loneliness are not only dealing with mental health challenges, but also with "increased risk of heart disease, dementia, depression, anxiety, sleep disturbances and even premature death."[129] Seeing that it is quite easy for those in rural areas, particularly the elderly and homebound, to experience loneliness, it makes the situation even more dire.

The pervasive nature of loneliness also underscores mental health as a critical need among rural Americans. As part of her team's research, McDonough and her BPC colleagues interviewed rural hospital leaders from around the country

---

128 Rural Health Information Hub, "Critical Access Hospitals (CAHs)."

129 Vivek Murthy, "Together: The Healing Power of Human Connection in a Sometimes Lonely World," Book website.

and learned that "the main thing that they needed to be dealing with was mental health."

Services like maternal and mental health are challenging to provide because they don't always contribute to the overall revenue of the hospital. Both maternal and mental health services are overwhelmingly paid by Medicaid, the medical insurance program for Americans living in poverty, resulting in lower reimbursement rates compared to services paid for by private insurers.

"When asking rural health leaders, 'if you had more money, what services would you want to offer?' they [all] said more mental health services across the board."

Coupled with a loss of economic opportunity, rural Americans were made easy targets during the opioid crisis that has ravaged the United States' small towns and agricultural areas in the past few years. According to the CDC, drug overdose death rates are higher in rural areas than in urban areas, with rural doctors being more likely to prescribe opioids more often.[130, 131] This increase in prescribing patterns in rural areas occurred against a backdrop of decreasing prescribing rates nationwide (starting in 2012).[132]

---

130 Centers for Disease Control and Prevention, "Drug overdose death rates are higher in rural areas than in urban areas," October 19, 2017.

131 Centers for Disease Control and Prevention, "Opioid Prescribing Rates in Nonmetropolitan and Metropolitan Counties Among Primary Care Providers Using an Electronic Health Record System -- United States, 2014 - 2017," *Morbidity and Mortality Weekly Report*, January 18, 2019.

132 Bram Sable-Smith and Wisconsin Public Radio, "Family Doctors In Rural America Tackle Crisis of Addiction and Pain," *Kaiser Health News*, January 10, 2020.

While there is a clear understanding of how specific phenomena, like the opioid crisis, have uniquely affected rural populations, other lifestyle and structural factors have an impact on rural health. According to Dr. Thomas Ricketts, professor at the University of North Carolina at Chapel Hill (UNC) Gillings School of Public Health and School of Medicine, some of the key health factors to consider include unique exposures to injuries and death associated with rural and industrial work, increased rates of drunk driving resulting in motor vehicle accidents causing death, poor water quality, and high levels of air pollution, especially if located near a coal mine.

In some ways, rural America is a different America, one where even physical access to clinical care is a challenge some find too difficult to overcome. So, what is one to do?

***

It is critical to understand the history of rural health which, while evolving alongside national conversations about health care access, still has its own trajectory. In an interview, Dr. Ricketts revealed that interest in rural health began in the 1970s, especially as more Americans began moving to urban areas. Dr. Ricketts himself did his doctoral dissertation in rural health practices in South Africa, which was quickly adapted for North Carolina. Around that same time, Jim Bernstein ensured that North Carolina was the first state to create an Office of Rural Health.

Jim Bernstein's extensive connections ensured this office was established through bipartisan support.[133] This office was one of the first in the United States that implemented visiting nurse services and deployed nurse practitioners from UNC and physician assistants from Duke University to serve as community-oriented primary care providers in the area.

Dr. Ricketts also outlined other examples of how rural health has come to the fore through the WWAMI Rural Health Research Centers, which is funded through the government agency Health Resources and Services Administration. WWAMI stands for Washington, Wyoming, Alaska, Montana, and Idaho, which are states with some of the largest rural populations in the United States. As regional rural health research centers gained increasing prominence, there was an eventual creation of the National Rural Health Association. Health became an increasingly relevant topic in rural areas as the number of small farms was decreasing.

Something that Dr. Ricketts stressed to me in our interview was that not all of rural America can be painted with the same broad brushstroke. Much like other marginalized communities, there are specific contexts within the rural experience that are necessary to understand, especially when considering health care needs. Dr. Ricketts put it best when he said,

"Rural America has a multicolored quilt of reality that somehow gets filtered down into a notion of, 'Hey, this is a rural thing.'"

---

133 Donald Madison MD, "The Work of James D. Bernstein of North Carolina," *North Carolina Journal of Medicine* 67, no. 1, January/February 2006.

A specific example that Dr. Ricketts shared of the different rural Americas came up when he described rural amenities. "The Department of Agriculture describes a rural amenity as having mountains, something for you to look at, rivers, lakes, a seaside or some other thing that's going to attract rich people to come and build second homes there."

Outside of the rural amenities regions, Dr. Ricketts also described the decline of small farms and stable rural employment because of mechanization. "You don't need as many people if you've got laser-guided tractors. The mechanization in tobacco that I'm familiar with now were not in machines in 1968. There were no machines that pick a backhoe; that was tough labor."

According to Dr. Ricketts, rural health care can only improve if there is a recognition of the value of community. Dr. Ricketts mentioned the strength of community, especially through faith-based organizations like church congregations, brings rural neighbors together.

"Church, in my understanding, in rural America, is where community happens, and it's where people take care of each other and where they take care of members of the community," Dr. Ricketts said. It is an understudied part of the social fabric in rural areas and should be tapped into when thinking about expanding access to health care in rural areas. When talking about his current experience living in rural North Carolina, Dr. Ricketts quipped,

"There are five churches that are within walking distance, all of which do some sort of social service. They have their own

community gardens and things like that… When I drive past the Methodist Church down the way, it's open porch day. Every Tuesday, people come and bring stuff, mostly canned food, and anybody can come and take it, no questions asked."

Dr. Ricketts points to the importance of leveraging strong community ties and building trust with health care institutions. For example, Richmond, Virginia-based Bon Secours Health System has established a Care-A-Van program, a mobile health clinic providing primary health services to uninsured adults and children. In some cases, Care-A-Van partners with local churches and religious organizations to build trust with populations that have large numbers of uninsured people.

For many years, advanced practitioners—licensed practice nurses (LPNs) and physician assistants (PAs)— served critical roles in rural health care settings where physicians were not always available. However, McDonough—herself a PA— noted LPNs and PAs are reimbursed at 85 percent of what a physician would be reimbursed. There are some exceptions to this, such as if the PA is practicing in the same space as a medical doctor. While cost effective and clinically efficient for the hospital, it may not help the hospital's financial bottom line to rely solely on these medical professionals to fill those shortages.

When asked about expanding the physician workforce in recognition of clinical shortages in rural areas, Dr. Ricketts mentioned an interesting approach:

"You can either be mercenary, by providing money as an incentive; missionary, by connecting physicians to church organizations; or military, by making rural practice part of obtaining a license, especially with the J-1 visa."

A story published by *Kaiser Health News* detailed the graduating class of University of Kansas School of Medicine-Salina, specifically dedicated to producing rural doctors.[134] The story followed a few of the students who graduated from this program to see where they chose to practice medicine. Some graduates, especially those who grew up in small rural towns, made good on their promise to practice medicine in rural areas. Dr. Tyson Wisinger, who grew up in the town of Phillipsburg with less than three thousand residents, was excited to go back to his hometown to practice medicine. Said Wisinger, "I can't have imagined a situation that could have been more rewarding."

Other incentives to practice rural medicine include becoming a pillar in the community where you live; more importantly, rural physicians become trusted resources and advisors for everyone facing health challenges in that town.

The story also highlights the biggest challenges of rural recruitment, including the lack of small-town residencies, spousal preferences on where to live, and the isolation that comes with practicing medicine alone. One graduate, Dr. Claire Hinrechsen Groskurth, wanted to practice in a more

---

134 Lauren Weber, "They Enrolled In Medical School To Practice Rural Medicine. What Happened?" *Kaiser Health News,* October 9, 2019.

rural setting, but after her spouse committed to specializing in surgery, she realized that they needed to live in a bigger city.

The challenge of practicing rural medicine is the stress of always having to be on call and being singularly responsible for the health of a town. Another graduate, Dr. Rany Gilpatrick, decided she wanted a more flexible outpatient schedule, free from the on-call life, and decided to settle in Topeka, Kansas (2018 population: 125,904).

The article also highlights the challenges of attracting newly minted doctors to rural areas in the first place. While the number of programs in medical schools geared toward rural medicine have increased dramatically—with support from the Department of Health Human Services, the 92 currently active rural health programs will increase to 119 over the next three years—unfortunate narratives have surrounded rural health. Many medical students are told early on that if they choose to practice rural medicine, they'll be overworked, underappreciated, and underpaid; this message is beaten into them repeatedly throughout their medical career.

While the Health Resources and Services Administration offers loan forgiveness for physicians practicing in rural areas, it is much more challenging to get those physicians to stay long term.[135]

---

135 U.S. Department of Health and Human Services. Health Resources & Services Administration, "NHSC Rural Community Loan Repayment Program."

In rural areas, according to Dr. Ricketts, the idea of the "good old family doctor" is rare because of high turnover. It's important to therefore consider underlying movements that physicians make across the country as a result. Moreover, Dr. Ricketts underscores that rural doctors should be matched based on town/regional need, not just the fact that these physicians want to practice in rural areas. If a particular town faces great challenges in diabetes and pain management, by deploying the appropriate physicians—primary care and pain specialists, for example—the people in that town can get the customized care they need in a timely fashion.

***

An extensive report published by the BPC covers research on the challenges rural community faces and how to meet their access needs in a cost-effective way.[136] The report, coauthored with former members of Congress and BPC staff, suggests four recommendations to address the fundamental challenges at the root of rural access issues:

- Tailoring health care services to fit community needs by generating flexible health care policies
- Ensuring that payment models and funding mechanisms reflect the reality of health care provision in rural areas, including smaller population and high operating costs
- Building out and maintaining the primary physician workforce, with the understanding physician shortages directly impact rural communities

---

136 Bipartisan Policy Center, "Bipartisan Policy Center."

- Expanding telemedicine services to ensure rural residents can access specialty care usually located in bigger cities.

These four areas highlight the need to stabilize and transform the rural health care infrastructure, from workforce, payments, and services perspectives. For example, with respect to tailoring health care services for specific communities, BPC urges stakeholders to consider clarifying rules around co-location so CAHs can partner with other kinds of health care providers. To fully recognize the reality of hospital care moving from inpatient to outpatient/same day care, CAH definitions need to be catered to the realities of outpatient care and reimbursed accordingly.

Moreover, BPC encourages different methods of building capacity among critical access hospitals and rural health care facilities. Given that these institutions are already stretched so thin, they should be given careful consideration when identifying the best ways to meet the needs of the populations they're serving. Such recommendations include:

- Developing a set of rural-specific quality measures and identifying ways to ensure proper reporting around those measures. This might be a long-term goal, using the existing templates of what is required to report for Medicare and reformatting for a rural context.
- Restructuring reimbursement incentives to make it easier for rural clinicians to move toward value-based care and also reduce administrative burden for these providers. This may require exempting certain services, like chronic care management, from beneficiary (insurance holder) cost-sharing through co-payments.

- Thoroughly utilizing the existing rural health care workforce by leveraging advanced practice nurses and physician assistants. Also expanding that workforce by providing loan exemptions for physicians practicing in the Indian Health Service and re-authorizing J-1 visas, which allow doctors to come from abroad to practice medicine in rural America.
- Seeing that broadband is now expanding in parts of rural America, actions such as including the patient's home as an authorized originating site for telehealth services and authorizing interstate telehealth interactions to promote access.

A lot of these recommendations are rooted in a few core ideas:

- Building off of existing policies—Using CMMI (Center for Medicare and Medicaid Innovation) specifications to determine what would be appropriate to make specific for rural health care facilities.
- Getting rid of policies that may not be working—Eliminating the US Drug Enforcement Administration (DEA) buprenorphine waiver requirement. Currently, physicians that want to prescribe buprenorphine have to go through eight hours of training and obtain a waiver before they are allowed to prescribe. Seeing that the opioid crisis predominantly affects rural communities, this policy seems like a bump in the road in terms of delivering life-saving care to those who need it.
- Establishing new policies and procedures—Establishing a new Rural and Emergency Outpatient Hospital designation. This would be helpful when recognizing current definitions around these designations are focused on

inpatient capacity, which runs contradictory to a reality in which a majority of procedures are shifting to the outpatient/same-day setting.

While many of these solutions have been built with the recognition that these communities are struggling with COVID-19, integrating these recommendations into mainstream practice for rural health can greatly allow an increase in access and ensure that policies are being implemented with rural realities in mind.

***

Like most communities, rural America is not a monolith. Different parts of rural America developed differently based on how industry has changed over time—tobacco in North Carolina, oil in Texas, and the mining industry in small towns in states like Montana and Wyoming. When closing out our interview, Dr. Ricketts pointed out,

"If you think of rural America as kind of a stuffy, old, unchanging place, the economics is incredibly dynamic. We were losing these [small] hospitals and starting clinics that were being supported by the federal government in the [individual] states, to a certain degree."

It is critical for us to remember the health care needs of those primarily regarded as living in "flyover zones." Unfortunately, "flyover" has become synonymous with "looked over." That should not be the case anymore.

Rural communities have struggled for a long time. Especially because of increasing mechanization and urbanization, rural populations have been dwindling and aging simultaneously. As hospitals and health systems have been downsizing and closing, those living in rural communities are continually left with fewer options to access health care.

However, there have been continued efforts to support those in rural areas. Whether it's through critical research conducted by people like Dr. Thomas Ricketts and institutions like the Bipartisan Policy Center or through backing from organizations like churches and nonprofits, rural health continues to be supported in ebbs and flows.

***

Rural economies have suffered for a long time given recent global and national trends, but also from a certain neglect of the rural population. This neglect has resulted in increasing poverty in rural areas.

Poverty, however, is not exclusive to America's small towns. It also persists in some of America's wealthiest cities.

What does poverty mean for access to health care?

CHAPTER 6

HOW THE OTHER HALF LIVES: POVERTY'S ROLE IN AMERICAN HEALTH CARE

"Long ago it was said that 'one half of the world does not know how the other half lives.' That was true then. It did not know because it did not care."

—JACOB RIIS, AMERICAN-DANISH JOURNALIST
AND AUTHOR OF *HOW THE OTHER HALF LIVES*

It is not surprising that people who make lower incomes have less access to quality health care compared to those who make more. By default, lower-income community members have less funds to purchase access to anything compared with their higher-income counterparts. This can include safe housing, clean drinking water, good public schools, and access to grocery stores and safe outdoor spaces. Dean

Sherry Glied of New York University's Wagner School of Public Service agrees that it's "hard to undo [that] fundamental inequality" because low-income and high-income families have different levels of resources, affecting what they can and cannot buy in any given marketplace.

However, that fundamental inequality has become intrinsic to the disparities we see in people's health care. In the United States, especially, beyond economics, political decisions drive how people are able to access quality health care.

The United States is one of the few developed nations in the world where employment is intrinsically linked to health care. The history behind this is clear. After the Great Depression and the start of World War II, hiring began to ramp up in an environment starved for employees, making those who were able to participate in the workforce a hot commodity. To prevent the few employees at home from job-hopping—which they were easily able to do, given how much employment choice they had—the National War Labor Board prevented an increase in workers' salaries in every industry—a salary cap—and also ruled that health insurance was exempt from this salary cap.[137]

This made health insurance an attractive benefit for employers to use to attract and retain new staff. To make things even better for employers, the Internal Revenue Service decided employer contributions to health insurance premiums were tax free, resulting in less out-of-pocket payments for workers.

---

137 Dan Gorenstein, "How did we end up with health insurance being tied to our jobs?" *Marketplace*, June 28, 2017.

While this system worked during wartime, it became challenging to maintain when soldiers returned to the workforce after the war was over. Additionally, there were almost no insurance provisions for the elderly, disabled, unemployed, or those who worked for employers who didn't provide insurance. This resulted in increasing efforts to create universal health care programs, starting from the Truman administration onwards.[138]

However, every time this push to expand coverage more universally was made, lobbying organizations, such as the American Medical Association, launched campaigns against these efforts. After attempts to quell any universal coverage program occurred in the 1950s under the Eisenhower administration, employer-based health care continues to be the de facto way to cover health insurance.

To be clear, private health insurance helped to dramatically increase health care coverage for working people. Through innovative insurance plans pioneered by the Blue Cross Blue Shield Association and Kaiser Permanente (and those like them), the percentage of the US population with health insurance jumped from 9.1 percent to 50.6 percent in the span of ten years.[139] However, sociologist Michael Harrington pointed to "another America," where 40 to 50 million citizens were "socially invisible" to the majority of the population and

138 Howard Markel, "69 years ago, a president pitches his idea for national health care," *PBS Newshour*, November 19, 2014.

139 Michael Morrissey, *Health Insurance: Second Edition* (Chicago: Health Administration Press, 2013), 3-25.

lacked access to basic medical care.[140] In his 1962 book, *The Other America,* Harrington defined those living in poverty as households of four people living with under $3,000 of annual income (almost $26,000 in 2020 dollars, which is roughly similar to the federal poverty line in 2020).[141] Around 8 million of those living in poverty were above the age of sixty-five.

1962 US Population Income Breakdown

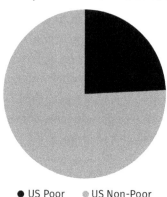

● US Poor   ● US Non-Poor

Source: US Census Bureau[142]; Michael Harrington, The Other America.[143]

It became clear that something needed to be done to ensure the poor and elderly could also have access to health insurance.

140 Rosemary Stevens, "Health Care in the Early 1960s," *Healthcare Financing Review* 15, no. 2 (1996): 11-22.

141 U.S. Department of Health & Human Services, Office of the Assistant Secretary for Planning and Evaluation, "Poverty Guidelines," 2020.

142 U.S. Census Bureau, "Statistical Abstract of the United States: 1962."

143 Michael Harrington, *The Other America* (New York City, Macmillan Publishers, 1962), 9-16.

***

So how did programs like Medicare and Medicaid come to exist?

Prior to 1965, Medicaid did not exist; if you were low income and were unable to afford any out-of-pocket costs, you and your family were simply in a difficult situation. However, President Lyndon B. Johnson recognized the scale of poverty that everyday Americans were experiencing.[144] Acknowledging that low income individuals did not have easy access to health insurance, President Johnson decided to tackle poverty by insuring this large swathe of the uninsured. As part of his War on Poverty, Medicaid was designed to provide health coverage to millions of Americans, including eligible low-income adults, pregnant women, children, elderly adults, and those with disabilities.[145]

Upon signing Medicare and Medicaid into law, President Johnson paid homage to President Truman's efforts by saying, "It was a generation ago that Harry Truman said, and I quote him: 'Millions of our citizens do not now have a full measure of opportunity to achieve and to enjoy good health. Millions do not now have protection or security against the economic effects of sickness.[146] And the time has now arrived for action to help them attain that opportunity and to help them get that protection.' Well, today, Mr. President, and my fellow Americans, we are taking such action—twenty years later."

---

144 History.com Editors, "Great Society," *History.com*, November 17, 2017.

145 U.S. Center for Medicare and Medicaid Services, "Medicaid," May 2020.

146 Tom van der Voort, "In The Beginning: Medicare and Medicaid," *UVA Miller Center,* July 24, 2017.

Much can be said about the value of expanding Medicaid access to marginalized communities. Medicaid is a government insurance program through which low income community members have access to health insurance. Along with Medicaid, the Children's Health Insurance Program was also passed, ensuring that children in low-income families also had access to health coverage. Per federal requirements, the program is funded both by state and federal governments. You need to be at a certain income level—which is typically 138 percent below the federal poverty line—in order to be eligible for Medicaid.[147]

While those might be federal guidelines, state governments have the freedom to set parameters for Medicaid eligibility however they see fit. This has meant that decisions around Medicaid have been drawn on political lines: states with more liberal governors overwhelmingly favor Medicaid expansion to cover a larger cohort of people. More conservative governors are in favor of a block grant-style program, which allows for the federal government to provide fixed grants to states while allowing states more flexibility in deciding who qualifies for Medicaid and for which services.[148]

Despite the installation of Medicaid, which arguably covers a large group of individuals who would otherwise be uninsured, current Medicaid definitions still leave out a lot of people. Given that many low-income individuals experience

147 U.S. Centers for Medicare and Medicaid Services, Healthcare.gov, "Federal Poverty Level (FPL)," May 2020.

148 Shefali Luthra, "Everything You Need To Know About Block Grants -- The Heart of GOP's Medicaid Plains," *Kaiser Health News,* January 24, 2017.

sporadic employment or promotions that may result in no longer meeting the Medicaid income requirement, many people fall in and out of Medicaid throughout their lives.

Much research has been done around the impact of Medicaid coverage on health care outcomes, including the concept of *expansion*. Medicaid expansion primarily occurs when the income ceiling for eligibility is raised to above the federal poverty level. Most recently, expansion of Medicaid coverage has been a centerpiece of the 2010 Affordable Care Act (ACA) until 2012, when the US Supreme Court let states choose whether they would like to expand Medicaid coverage.[149] That decision has had significant impact.

In a comparative study done by Kaiser Health News, it was found that state borders can have a huge impact on who is insured and who is not.[150] The study followed a middle-aged woman, Patricia Powers, who was uninsured in Missouri. Although she previously had health insurance through her husband's employment, she stopped receiving consistent coverage when her husband became disabled in 2009.

While he was eventually able to receive Medicare, she and her husband were unable to qualify for subsidies on the federal ACA marketplace, resulting in her having to go without insurance. Given her lack of insurance, she remained unaware of the cancerous tumors growing in her breasts. Had she lived across the Mississippi River in Illinois, she

---

149 Medicaid and CHIP Payment and Access Commission, "Changes in coverage and access."

150 Laura Ungar, "The Deep Divide: State Borders Create Medicaid Haves and Have-Nots," *Kaiser Health News,* October 2, 2019.

would have been eligible for Medicaid because of Illinois' decision to expand Medicaid. Some policy leaders in Missouri, like the Director of Government Accountability for the Show-Me Institute Patrick Ishmael, believe that Medicaid expansion would drain resources and increase taxpayer costs. Budget-wise, it is difficult to tell what would happen if Missouri expanded Medicaid, which is highly contingent on how many people sign up.

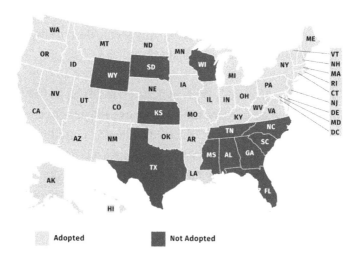

Map of which states adopted Medicaid expansion, and which ones did not. Updated most recently on August 17, 2020.[151] Source: Kaiser Family Foundation

***

151 "Status of State Action on the Medicaid Expansion Decision," *Kaiser Family Foundation.*

It is important to recognize, however, that Medicaid is not the panacea to improve health outcomes among lower-income populations. While insurance coverage remains a challenge—for example, many like Patricia Powers have incomes too low to qualify for ACA marketplace subsidies but too high to be eligible for Medicaid without expansion—health coverage remains only one component in the improvement of quality of life.

According to Dr. Sherry Glied, addressing issues of access to care is not difficult. In an interview, Glied said, "It's actually a pretty easy answer, which is you have to give people coverage and the coverage has to be good enough that they can get access to services that work." It is still unknown how to best address the social determinants of health, such as housing or income support, that have huge impacts on health outcomes themselves.

The reminder of this inequality was made clear during a powerful testimony given by Amy Jo Hutchison at the House Oversight and Reform Subcommittee on Government Operations.[152] As an organizer for working class community members from West Virginia, Hutchison argued to encourage Congress to update the federal poverty guidelines that recognize the realities of poor, working class Americans—which would ultimately impact their Medicaid eligibility.

Explaining her financial situation to members of Congress, Hutchison made clear that despite holding two jobs and a

---

152 D.K. Wright, "West Virginia woman's plea to Congress makes national news," *ABC 4,* February 13, 2020.

bachelor's degree, she had to make difficult financial decisions every day—how much to buy in groceries, what money to spend to allow her daughter to go on a band trip, which bills to ignore to ensure that she could be on Capitol Hill that day. However, according to Federal Poverty Guidelines, she is not considered poor.

An example she gave was that the federal poverty guidelines suggest that a family of three has to make below $21,720. If the head of household makes $22,000 a year (making that person ineligible for assistance) and pays $1,200 a month in rent, they are left with $8,000 for food, transportation, and other costs for the year.

That comes out to $166 a week.

Clearly not enough.

In her testimony, she shared the story of a single mom she had met who was recently promoted to manager of a grocery store. After she reported her new income to the West Virginia Department of Health and Human Resources, her rent almost doubled. Due to her new income, she lost her SNAP (Supplemental Nutrition Assistance Program) benefits and her family's health insurance.

Unfortunately, this resulted in her resignation and going back to her previous position so her family could survive. In a country where employment and health care insurance are inextricably linked, certain increases in income make individuals and their families ineligible for Medicaid but too poor to afford private health care. Therefore, they are faced with two choices, equally challenging, with no sign of upward mobility in sight.

"Poverty rolls off the backs of parents and right onto our children despite how hard we try."

AMY JO HUTCHISON, NORTHERN REGIONAL ORGANIZER FOR WV HEALTHY KIDS AND FAMILIES COALITION

In many cases, these choices also result in parents slipping into habits that worsen health to better provide for their children. Hutchison related how she had given up dinner on many nights so her children could have enough to eat, and how her lack of health insurance—despite being employed full time as a Head Start teacher—resulted in her relying on "essential oils and prayers" to take care of her gall bladder.

***

These important realizations can make the current climate for improving health outcomes for low-income individuals quite grim. As Linda Tirado points out in her gripping piece from *The Guardian,* low-income individuals struggle with multiple facets of their life—from unemployment or underemployment to inability to access nutritional food—so another solution starts to become clearer. While coordinating social services may be considered one potential tool to improve quality of life, Dr. Sherry Glied describes what the research shows:

"When you coordinate services at a very, very microscale, at the level, say, a social worker who helps a family to navigate multiple different systems, you can do better. However, if you're not sure any of these services work, perhaps coordinating them is not the way to go."

While coordination of social services seems like a nice, go-to answer, what really deserves focus is strengthening the efficiency and capacity of these social service programs. This has become increasingly critical as more and more Americans are suffering downward economic mobility because of market trends and the COVID-19 pandemic.

In a *CNN Money* article, Tirado emphasized the sheer invisibility of low-income community members by saying, "It is millions of us. You can't go through a day without seeing us and yet we somehow still don't exist."[153] The COVID-19 pandemic highlighted some of the challenges of low-income workers, many of whom were deemed essential, including their inability to quarantine safely or access health care once they were experiencing symptoms. In a searing piece, *The New York Times* interviewed members of the Queens community—many of whom had professions such as taxi driver, Uber driver, nanny, and restaurant worker, among others—who identify as immigrants and have been candid about their health care experiences.[154]

---

153   Patrick Gillespie, "Linda Tirado: What I miss about being poor," *CNN Money,* October 2, 2014.

154   Annie Correal and Andrew Jacobs, "'A Tragedy Is Unfolding': Inside New York's Virus Epicenter," *The New York Times,* April 9, 2020. Updated August 5, 2020.

Those made most invisible—low income immigrants in particular—have suffered the most during this crisis. Unable to work from home or get leniency on rent, these people struggle with staying afloat.

***

When you first see a photo of Linda Tirado, she looks like what you'd expect an American adult in her early thirties to look like. A bobbed haircut and a warm smile are the most common features you see when you look up a photo of her. But what you wouldn't know is that responding to a simple forum question was all it took to put her on the map.

After a grueling day working a several-hour shift, Linda saw a question on the blogging website Kinja asking why people living in poverty behaved in seemingly self-destructive ways.[155] After thinking through her experiences, along with others, growing up and living in poverty, she penned a few paragraphs and hit "submit." In a matter of weeks, her response was shared thousands of times online, resulting in her post being republished on sites like *The Guardian* and *Huffington Post*.[156] Linda finally wrote a book about her experiences living in poverty and what folks in middle class America don't understand, entitled *Hand to Mouth: Living in Bootstrap America*.

---

155 Kinja, "Users following Kinja blog."
156 Linda Tirado, "This Is Why Poor People's Bad Decisions Make Perfect Sense," *Huffington Post*, November 22, 2013. Updated December 6, 2017.

Through a combination of her own narrative, the stories of others, and facts, Tirado paints a moving picture of the challenges Americans in poverty experience. Typically juggling multiple jobs, Tirado explains the challenge of planning financially or socially for the future. Americans living in poverty typically have difficulty accessing healthy foods and may not have the time or resources to put together healthy meals. "Junk food," Tirado highlights, "is a pleasure that we are allowed to have; why would we give that up?"

Poor folks in the United States have challenges establishing bank accounts, which means hours of time spent figuring out how to cash a check or getting money orders to pay bills. The nature of the work that poor people do does not respect their time and ability. Jobs in fast food and retail are often highly unscheduled, resulting in inability to plan for things like childcare or going back to school. Moreover, people in poverty are more likely to work temporary jobs in which they do not receive regular employment and benefits. This continues to exacerbate the cycle of poverty that these community members experience.

Why, many ask, do poor people in America make poor financial decisions? Should they not know better and save for the future? Tirado's compelling counterpoint is "none of them [financial decisions] matter, in the long term. I will never not be poor, so what does it matter if I don't pay a thing and a half this week instead of just one more thing?" Especially when that "thing" you're looking to spend money on is fast food—cheap, convenient, and accessible—what is the harm in getting another Big Mac?

In Tirado's statement about being poor and staying poor, the common cultural narrative of the American Dream and upward mobility crumbles. Tirado makes it clear that people like her have never believed in the American Dream. In Tirado's words, while upward mobility feels permanently blocked, "the layer between lower-middle class and poor is horrifyingly porous from above."

Tirado also overcomes many common arguments made against the poor, such as "why don't they try harder to find jobs that will pay more?" Connecting physical appearance to better jobs is part of her thesis, indicating that poverty can result in missing teeth or yellowing skin, which can impact the types of roles one can apply for. Words like "fitting into the corporate image" may indeed be code for "needing to be beautiful enough to get the job." In a searing statement, Tirado says, "Beauty is a thing you get when you can afford it, and that's how you get the job that you need in order to be beautiful. There isn't much point trying."

The underscoring point of Tirado's work, however, is that poor people, too, want to be valued for the work that they do and seen as contributors to society. Ironically, during the COVID-19 pandemic that ravaged the globe earlier this year, Americans living in poverty held our society together. Their jobs as grocery store cashiers, sanitation workers, hospital orderlies, fast food and restaurant workers, and custodial team members is what has allowed most Americans to continue their lives during that time. In an interview with *CNN*, Tirado said about poor, working class Americans, "You can't go through a day without seeing us and yet we somehow still don't exist. All work has dignity."

While Tirado provides a poignant narrative perspective on poverty in America, research supports the challenges that low-income individuals face in accessing health care. According to a paper published by *Health Affairs*, low-income workers are more likely to be uninsured, less likely to receive new drugs or technology, and less likely to have ready access to primary and specialty care.[157] Without health insurance, low-income workers are more likely to forgo regular medical care because of cost concerns. While Medicaid, a predominantly state-funded program that provides health care for Americans at a certain level above the federal poverty line, can provide some respite for poor Americans, it has not addressed the issue of access wholesale. Much like the Affordable Care Act, Medicaid addresses only the issue of insurance coverage and not of improving overall health.

Low Income Workers' Health Insurance Status (2016)

● Low Income, Receives Health Insurance through Employer

● Low Income, Does Not Receive Health Insurance through Employer

---

157 Dhruv Khullar and Dave Chokshi, "Health, Income, & Poverty: Where We Are & How We Can Help," *Health Affairs*, October 4, 2018.

High Income Workers' Health Insurance Status (2016)

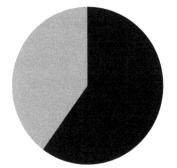

● High Income, Receives
Health Insurance

◉ High Income, Does Not Receive Health
Insurance through Employer

Source: Kaiser Family Foundation[158]

From a hospital visit perspective, people in poverty avoid seeking even routine health care. According to health care research organization The Commonwealth Fund, even if they are insured, they need to forgo much-needed wages to take time to see a doctor.[159] Moreover, they also need to find someone to watch their children and a way to get to their physician. From a lifestyle perspective, poor Americans are more likely to live in neighborhoods that don't have access to healthy produce or safe areas to walk around or play outside, also contributing to negative health.

158 Alanna Williamson, Larisa Antonisse, Jennifer Tolbert, Rachel Garfield, and Anthony Damico, "ACA Coverage Expansions and Low-Income Workers," *Kaiser Family Foundation,* June 10, 2016.

159 Shanoor Seervai, "It's Harder for People Living in Poverty to Get Health Care," *The Commonwealth Fund,* April 19, 2019.

Therefore, recommendations to promote healthy behaviors may not work easily with low-income patients, given their circumstances. Commonwealth Fund researcher Corinne Lewis recalled a patient who said, "I can't take my kids to play outside where we live. We have to go to a different neighborhood. Because where we live, there's broken glass on the streets. There's dirt everywhere. There are constant car break-ins. There are people doing drugs."

The patient being interviewed closed her story on a poignant note, "It's because we're at the bottom of the totem pole." In this patient's eyes, who was going to care about the issues of daily living that produced the negative health outcomes she and her family faced anyway?

***

While the above are unfortunate facts of life in poverty in America, the recurring issue with low-income patients is building trust with their provider. After interviewing hundreds of low-income patients, Lewis pointed out that most of these patients, particularly those of color, felt judged or that they were being discriminated against. Lewis recalled the story of one particular patient sharing what a doctor said to her about her substance abuse problem, obesity, and diabetes and feeling judged and disrespected.

Understanding the history of Medicaid and Medicare—the closest that America has come to "socialized medicine"—is critical to understanding why health care continues to feel out of reach for low-income Americans, including undocumented people. While Medicaid in particular is designed on a state-by-state basis—the states famously considered "the laboratories of democracy"—it may not always ensure that their care is covered at all times.[160]

In many ways, it feels as if the health care cards are stacked against low-income populations. Tirado mentions that downward mobility is a real fear among Americans hovering just above the poverty line, indicating that it is just like quicksand: "Once it grabs you, it keeps constraining your options until it's got you completely." This is especially true of essential workers during COVID-19, who are realizing more and more that they are not essential; they are sacrificial.[161]

This is Tirado's whole point to begin with.

But now, people are starting to pay attention. Even more importantly, while policy and shifting cultural attitudes have been mainstay solutions in alleviating health disparities, the technology sector has become a place that the health care industry can increasingly turn to for solutions.

---

160 Bradley Blakeman, "States are the laboratories of democracy," *The Hill*, May 7, 2020.
161 Sujatha Gidla, "'We Are Not Essential. We Are Sacrificial," *The New York Times*, May 5, 2020.

PART FOUR

BRINGING PAST MOVEMENTS TO THE FORE

CHAPTER 7

THE "FAIRER SEX": NAVIGATING HEALTH CARE AS WOMEN

––––

"When women take care of their health,
they become their best friend."
—POET AND AUTHOR MAYA ANGELOU

"But why won't they just believe me?"

Through tears, your friend tells you about the chronic pain she has experienced as someone with endometriosis. The constant pain in her lower stomach, the inability to overcome the perpetual fatigue, and regular feelings of nausea don't seem to go away for her. She has tried several times to communicate with her physician about how her pain has been worsening over time but has been readily dismissed each time. The recurring refrain has been, "Well, that's what happens with this condition."

Your friend's story is not unique, nor is it unique to biologically female conditions like endometriosis. Shortly after completing her bachelor's degree at Carleton College, journalist and author Maya Dusenbery started experiencing increasing pain in her joints. She was promptly diagnosed with rheumatoid arthritis and prescribed the appropriate medications.

Quickly, however, Dusenbery learned that was not the experience of many women. In fact, many women are not taken seriously when they first report their pain and are often misdiagnosed or not diagnosed at all. This is especially exacerbated for women of color.

Dusenbery found stories that corroborated this research. In her work as a journalist, she came across the story of Diane Talbert.[162] Talbert is a Black woman from a small town in Virginia. She had been diagnosed with severe psoriasis as a child but continued to battle with severe pain throughout her life. In her twenties, she was unable to lift her hands above her head but was told at a doctor's appointment that the pain was all in her head. Later in life, her pain was mistakenly attributed to signs of early menopause.

Not until her late fifties did a physician take her pain seriously and diagnose her with psoriatic arthritis.

Unfortunately, stories like Talbert's are not unique. Gender bias in medicine has a history that started a much longer time ago.

---

162 Maya Dusenbery, "'All In Your Head?' Getting Care for Untreated Pain," *Consumer Reports,* May 2, 2019.

***

According to famed Greek philosopher Aristotle, females are nothing more than mutilated males.[163] While the origin of this thought occurred centuries ago, this belief has persisted in medical culture in Western society. Gender bias specific to pain perception can easily be traced back to Darwinism, where white, European men were considered most superior.

Dr. Amanda Williams, reader in clinical health psychology at University College London, posits, "Black people endured horrendous hardship and brutality, so it was said that they were less sensitive to pain, and women endured childbirth, which was pretty painful, so it was believed that they were oversensitive, prone to hysterics."

Ultimately, it has resulted in a medical health care system designed by men, for men. According to Australian public health researcher Dr. Kate Young, women who returned to the doctor time and time again because treatments weren't effective for them weren't left with much choice.[164]

"Rather than acknowledge the limitations of medical knowledge, medicine expected women to take control (with their minds) of their disease (in their body) by accepting their illness, making 'lifestyle' changes and conforming to their gendered social roles of wife and mother," Dr. Young stated in an interview with *The Guardian*.[165] Women who were

163 Goodreads, "Aristotle > Quotes."
164 Gabrielle Jackson, "The female problem: how male bias in medical trials ruined women's health," *The Guardian*, November 13, 2019.
165 Ibid.

unable to make such lifestyle changes were condemned as irresponsible and hysterical, a belief that has unfortunately persisted to present day.

Furthermore, women's reproductive functions were used not only as a tool for policing women's sexual behavior, but also as reason for the development of certain diseases. For example, women suffering from endometriosis were told childbearing at an older age was the cause; those with breast cancer were told pregnancy would be the cure. Without well-founded scientific research, physicians continued to support mainstream conversations around women's responsibilities to society: having healthy children at an early age. If they could not fulfill that societal duty, the result was "suffering from disease."

An extension of that argument is pervasive in rhetoric surrounding current abortion debates. Many reproductive justice advocates argue that women's bodies continue to be policed by the federal government and certain state governments. The book *Obstacle Course: The Everyday Struggle to Get an Abortion in America* highlights the challenges that women face in obtaining an abortion, including, in certain states, having mandated waiting periods or being told false-hoods by doctors.[166]

Law professor Michele Goodwin highlights the ways in which health care laws and policies coerce women, particularly those who are poor and of color. In fact, according to

---

166 Amazon, "Obstacle Course: The Everyday Struggle to Get an Abortion in America."

The Washington Post, Goodwin posits the idea that "women's bodies are treated as property of the state and of men, who make up the large majority of legislators and who write and apply the laws."[167]

More often than not, in health care, women are reduced to being men with "boobs and tubes."[168] At least, that's according to Dr. Alyson McGregor, who is now world renowned in studying the medical differences between men and women. "Women's health" is normally associated strictly with reproductive health, and not with things we know now to be true— that women having heart attacks present differently from men.

Indeed, when Dr. McGregor was asked what she would like to specialize in after completing training in emergency medicine, she responded "women's health." It wasn't long before she became everyone's point of contact for pelvic examinations in women.

In her new book *Sex Matters*, Dr. McGregor highlights how much about women's health we don't know. According to a profile of Dr. McGregor's work in *The Guardian*, we often hear talk of "personalized medicine" and "targeted therapies," but those breakthroughs are vastly disparate compared to the very little that's been done to understand how women respond to different treatments and procedures.[169] That has

---

167 Katha Pollitt, "The long fight for reproductive rights is only getting harder," *The Washington Post*, May 13, 2020.

168 Anna Moore, "Why does medicine treat women like men?", *The Guardian*, May 24, 2020.

169 Ibid.

bred surprise and frustration; McGregor has said, "That's a common reaction. I often hear, 'Gosh, I thought medicine was taking this into account!'"

Both Dr. McGregor's and Dusenbery's interest in gender bias in medicine grew in three realms:

- In her research, Dusenbery learned that women's symptoms for mainstream conditions such as heart disease were not well understood or researched.
- Diseases that predominantly affect women—such as fibromyalgia and vulvodynia (chronic pain in the vulvar area)—are not effectively researched or understood.
- The impact of chronic disease on women is much more severe given that they are most likely to take on unpaid domestic labor to care for loved ones and are most likely to not have social supports when they are going through the same illness.

***

From a policy standpoint, Dusenbery recognized that health care policies and protocols were overwhelmingly set and decided by men. In the process of her research, Dusenbery uncovered some shocking information that was alarmingly aligned with the above, setting research on women's health behind by decades.

The first was that the Food and Drug Administration (FDA) was concerned for a long time with the impact of clinical trials on women and their potential fetuses, resulting in the

FDA banning women of reproductive age from participating in such trials.[170]

Even today, women's bodies are viewed by medicine primarily as reproductive bodies. (Recall "boobs and tubes.") Since reproductive organs were considered the primary distinguishing marker between men and women, medical leaders did not think to study how female bodies might be physiologically different. Moreover, given that women are born with all the eggs they will ever produce, they were systematically excluded from all drug trials, regardless of their wish or ability to bear children.

As a result, according to Associate Director for Women's Health research at the National Institutes of Health Dr. Janine Austin Clayton, "We literally know less about every aspect of female biology compared to male biology."

In *Sex Matters*, Dr. McGregor meticulously lays out how today's drugs are still failing women. This has to do with the fact that women metabolize drugs differently because of hormones and enzymes, which is not considered when those drugs are prescribed or when advisory warnings are designed for over-the-counter drugs. A great example of this is how Ambien—a well-known sleeping pill—is metabolized differently in male and female bodies, which can sometimes have fatal consequences.

---

170 Terry Gross, "How 'Bad Medicine' Dismisses And Misdiagnoses Women's Symptoms," March 27, 2018, in *Fresh Air*, produced by Heidi Saman and Seth Kelley, podcast, MP3 audio, 19:17.

A specific example that Dr. McGregor lays out is the impact of medication on the resting time between heartbeats—known as QT. Women have longer QTs than men do, and some prescription drugs cause incremental QT increases as a side effect. Dr. McGregor's *Guardian* profile details, "For women on multiple meds (and statistically, women are most likely to be on multiple meds), the risk of these combined increases can range from simple arrhythmia to sudden cardiac death."

However, inadvertently, women were also excluded from observational studies about topics such as aging. A stark example of this is how heart disease has been studied and researched in the United States. While men and women alike may complain of chest pain or discomfort, there is a higher likelihood of women not experiencing this symptom. Women may present different symptoms from men, resulting in younger women, such as those under age fifty-five, being seven times more likely to get sent home from the hospital while their heart attack is in progress. As a result, data regarding basic facets of women's health are lagging decades behind compared to that of men.

In 1993, the National Institutes for Health (NIH) were mandated by Congress to include women in their research studies.[171] While this helped increase female representation in NIH studies, it is still not the norm to compare differences between genders to better understand how diseases and conditions might present differently. This is especially true when it comes to including pregnant women in

---

171 Ibid.

studies. There may be cases in which a pregnant woman is prescribed a drug that has never been studied in pregnancy. In this respect, women continue to be let down by federal health care policy.

***

Dusenbery found this lack of attention to diseases predominantly affecting women to be rooted in a systemic bias against women reporting their pain results. This bias has also widely been known as the "trust gap" that physicians have with female patients.[172] The "trust gap" basically states that when a woman's physical symptoms don't easily align with a diagnosis or a condition, the woman's psychological condition was to be blamed.

This idea of women being "hysterical" about the pain they experience dates back to the eighteenth and nineteenth centuries. When it came to pain particular to women-specific conditions such as endometriosis, childbirth, or menstrual cramps, according to President and CEO of the Society for Women's Health Research, Amy Miller, it became common for women to be told that "their pain is just a normal part of being a woman."

---

172 Jenara Nerenberg, "How to Address Gender Inequality in Health Care," *Greater Good Magazine*, March 9, 2018.

Women and Autoimmune Disease
(2018)

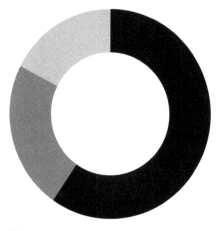

- ● 59.9 % Population without Autoimmune Disease
- ● 22.9% Population with Autoimmune Disease
- ● 17.2% Women with Autoimmune Disease

Source: Greater Good Magazine.[173]

Dr. McGregor's research also corroborates this. Epidemiological studies indicate that women are at greater risk of pain conditions, including migraines, irritable bowel syndrome (IBS), premenstrual syndrome (PMS), and others. This may be in part due to the ways in which sex hormones, neurotransmitters, and central nervous systems interact within female bodies. Women are also more likely to develop autoimmune diseases because of the double-X chromosome—while those chromosomes create aggressive immune responses in fighting disease, they are also more likely to turn on the body itself.

---

173 Ibid.

When women are experiencing pain, regardless of its cause, they are more likely to receive a psychiatric diagnosis compared to a physical one. According to Dr. Williams, "Women are prescribed less analgesic. When a man says that he's in a bit of pain, we think he's really in a lot of pain. When a woman says she's in a lot of pain, we think she's in a bit of pain, but worried about it."

Given that women are told by physicians so regularly that their pain isn't real, Dusenbery uncovered another disturbing fact: many women "felt that bringing a partner or a father or even a son would be helpful. And then [they] found that it was [helpful], that they were treated differently when there was that man in the room who was corroborating their reports." Sadly, this was true regardless of the gender of the doctor. While these accounts of bringing a male relative to increase legitimacy have been commonly heard in places like car dealerships and automotive shops, the doctor's office is the last place where this legitimacy should be necessary. According to Dusenbery, "the roots of the problem are in unconscious bias and systemic bias." It is not that doctors don't want to help their patients; it is the assumptions that are being made about certain types of patients that promote harm.

In some cases, that bias can have fatal consequences.

***

"We usually see women prioritizing the health of their family members over their own health. However, as the health of families and communities is dependent on the health of women, it is critically important that women be supported to engage in that care."

DR. ONI BLACKSTOCK, FORMER ASSISTANT COMMISSIONER OF NYC DEPARTMENT OF HEALTH AND CLINICAL ASSISTANT PROFESSOR AT ALBERT EINSTEIN COLLEGE OF MEDICINE

A shocking study published in the summer of 2018 indicated that women are less likely to survive a heart attack when treated by a male physician.[174] The study was led by Laura Huang of Harvard Business School, who had previously studied racial and gender bias in workplace hiring and entrepreneurship. While the paper did not look into health care outcomes based on race or gender identity (including nonbinary people), previous research indicates that women of color, LGBTQ+ women, and gender-nonconforming people have had negative experiences with being taken seriously by their physicians.

An article in *Rewire News* profiling the study, highlights the poignant story of Florida-based twenty-seven-year old Annalise Mabe, who was routinely disrespected by a male OB/GYN joking about her sexual assault and conducting an annual exam without her consent.[175] Mabe shared that, generally, male doctors had been condescending and dismissive.

---

174 Brad N. Greenwood, Seth Carnahan, and Laura Huang, "Patient-physician gender concordance and increased mortality among female heart attack patients," *Proceedings of the National Academy of Sciences of the United States of America* 115, no. 24 (2018): 8569-8574.

175 Julissa Trevino, "New Paper Examines How Gender Bias in Health Care Can Be Deadly," *Rewire News*, October 4, 2018.

"If I bring up research, they assume I looked it up on WebMD," she shared with *Rewire News*.

It is completely sensible to ask here: Why do we continue *not* to believe women? And why does this apply even more so to women of color? According to Dr. Salimah Meghani, past chair of the American Pain Society's Pain Disparities Special Interest Group, "A lot of work in the social sciences has shown that you're more empathetic to people in your in-group than your out-group."[176] Given that doctors are majority-white and still male in the United States, it's not a surprise that women and minorities are not believed when they report pain. Meghani also points out there is currently no objective way to measure and manage pain. This results in clinicians having a more challenging time trusting patients who do not look like them to report their pain "accurately," and vice versa.

Dusenbery's last leg of research has included how women overall have been impacted by chronic disease. Overwhelmingly, women have taken the responsibility to be caretakers of family members with Alzheimer's. According to the Shriver Report and Alzheimer's Association, a survey indicated that half of women caring for someone with Alzheimer's are providing more than forty hours of care a week.[177] This unpaid care work is the "work that makes all other work possible," according to Dusenbery's reporting. However, her reporting also uncovered that women in their seventies are

---

176 Consumer Reports, "Is bias keeping female, minority patients from getting proper care for their pain?" *The Washington Post*, July 29, 2019.

177 The Shriver Report, "A Woman's Nation Takes On Alzheimer's," October 2010.

twice as likely to get Alzheimer's as their male counterparts. Unfortunately, at that point, women are more likely to be widowed and not have the social supports necessary to get through Alzheimer's at home.[178] For this reason, women rely more on Medicaid—they are more likely to be poor in old age—and more often live in nursing homes than their male counterparts.

Women's economic and domestic contributions are critical to the backbone of American society and economy. However, they have been systematically left out of critical conversations about health care diagnoses and treatments. Most importantly, women are the ones who bear the brunt of caregiving for the elderly, sick, and the very young, but they are also the ones who economically and socially lose the most in the process.

While the above information is incredibly saddening, it is nonetheless not very surprising. Centuries of not taking women seriously, stripping women of their rights, and policing women's bodies have naturally created a medical system that is still unequipped to deal with women's medical challenges in a respectful way. For now, many female patients suffering from bias and misdiagnosis have been forced to become super advocates for themselves and others like them. The onus should not always be on the woman suffering to educate her physician on her physiological differences and to convince her physician that her pain is worthy of being examined.

---

178 Maya Dusenbery, "Compared to Men, Women Bear Six Times More of the Cost of Alzheimer's Disease," *Pacific Standard*, June 14, 2017.

According to *Duke Health*, physicians can do small things to better understand and overcome their biases in patient interactions.[179] Beyond hiring diverse health care teams, one of the most straightforward solutions is deploying checklists and guidelines. Regardless of the gender of the patient, by ensuring the same questions are routinely asked during certain care episodes—like an annual primary care visit—patients of different genders can expect to receive the same treatment. Using open-ended questions to allow for patients to bring up concerns that physicians may not have otherwise considered can be helpful in centering the patient in their care episode. A simple "What are your concerns today? What am I missing that is important for us to talk about?" can go a long way.

For too long, a top-down approach has not worked in creating transformational change in medicine for women. The purpose behind Dr. McGregor's book, *Sex Matters,* is to empower and educate women. Some of the specific advice in the book for female patients ranges from "volunteering for medical trials to researching sex differences in prescriptions, recording side-effects, joining patient support groups, keeping careful records of symptoms, and taking an advocate along to appointments." According to Dr. McGregor, "If you look at past experiences, it took great grassroots efforts to have women's reproductive health taken seriously."

In Dusenbery's words, the true solution in tackling bias and making medicine more inclusive for female patients lies within.

---

179 Emily Paulsen, "Recognizing, Addressing Unintended Gender Bias in Patient Care," *Duke Health*, October 9, 2019.

"I hope patient advocacy can help birth changes, but that people within medicine will really take on this problem. They're the ones who we need to fix it."

It is clear women have been marginalized in most, if not all, of their health care experiences. Whether it is not being included in key studies, not being listened to in doctors' appointments, or not being believed when in pain, women have faced incredible challenges in ensuring that the care they receive is equitable and high quality. A combination of (incorrect) cultural narratives about women being inferior—but also simultaneously more able to withstand pain—and women being left out of important studies and medical conversations has led to this point. Moreover, cultural expectations around women caring for others when they are ill—a child with a stuffy nose, a parent with a recently replaced hip, a sibling struggling with depression—results in further challenges when those very women become ill.

***

At present, there is much that female patients can do to reclaim their health care experiences and push back against physicians—by asking the right questions, by advocating for their needs based on their specific chronic condition, by volunteering to be part of clinical trials so side effects in women can be more appropriately studied. But what about clinicians and the health care system that supports them?

While unlearning bias is incredibly difficult—especially if you've been trained by a system in which those biases are so deeply rooted—clinical staff has the responsibility to ensure they are checking and recognizing those biases. Most importantly, data aggregation on the basis of gender is key. COVID-19 has taught all of the United States about the disproportionate effects health crises can have on marginalized communities—namely people of color. However, Dr. McGregor argues the need to collect health data by sex as well: "I'm trying to create a call for all countries to start collecting COVID-19 data by sex so that we can have this knowledge ahead of time. In the H1N1 [swine flu] pandemic, it wasn't until we started looking at sex differences that we realized pregnant women were very susceptible to complications."[180]

Women in the United States have a history of organizing around issues that they care about. Whether it was the abolition of slavery, women's suffrage, women's liberation, or civil rights, women have been both at the forefront and behind the scenes, organizing and strategizing.

Dr. McGregor and Dusenbery have already shown that medical treatment is the next big frontier.

---

180 Anna Moore, "Why does medicine treat women like men?", *The Guardian*, May 24, 2020.

CHAPTER 8

HERE, QUEER & WITHOUT FEAR: LGBTQ+ ACCESS TO HEALTH CARE

———

"I'm not missing a minute of this. It's a revolution!"
—SYLVIA RIVERA, LATINA TRANS WOMAN AND LGBTQ+
ACTIVIST ACTIVE DURING THE STONEWALL UPRISING

Explanatory Note: The acronym LGBTQ+ refers to individuals who identify as lesbian, gay, bisexual, transgender, and queer. According to the Human Rights Campaign, the United States' largest civil rights organization dedicated to advocating on behalf of the LGBTQ+ community, here are the definitions of the different parts of the initialism.

Lesbian: A woman who is emotionally, romantically, or sexually attracted to other women.

Gay: A person who is emotionally, romantically, or sexually attracted to members of the same gender.

Bisexual: A person emotionally, romantically, or sexually attracted to more than one sex, gender, or gender identity, though not necessarily simultaneously, in the same way or to the same degree.

Transgender: An umbrella term for people whose gender identity and/or expression is different from cultural expectations based on the sex they were assigned at birth. Being transgender does not imply any specific sexual orientation. Therefore, transgender people may identify as straight, gay, lesbian, bisexual, etc.

Cisgender: Although not reflected in the acronym, it is necessary to understand this term in relation to transgender people. Cisgender individuals are those whose gender identity and/or expression is the same as cultural expectations based on the sex they were assigned at birth.

The "+" signifies other gender identities and sexual orientations not reflected in the acronym.

For many Americans, the LGBTQ+ community gained visibility in two historical moments: the Stonewall riots that took place at the end of the 1960s and the HIV/AIDS epidemic, which took the lives of many young LGBTQ+ community members in the 1980s. However, this community has always been in existence in the United States; the first documented

US gay rights organization—the Society for Human Rights—was founded in 1924 by Henry Gerber.[181]

The first lesbian rights organization, the Daughters of Bilitis, was started in 1955 in San Francisco.[182] As the Netflix documentary *A Secret Love* can attest, frequenting gay and lesbian bars and clubs was the best way to build community and find friendships among like-minded people living similar lifestyles. However, these establishments were frequently raided by the police, resulting in arrests, loss of employment, and loss of reputation for those who were caught.[183]

It was a similar raiding of the Stonewall Inn, located in Greenwich Village in New York City, that resulted in riots between the gay community and the police force.[184] While the Genovese crime family paid off New York's Sixth Police Precinct to ignore the activities at Stonewall Inn, this did not last; police came in on the morning of June 28, physically harassed patrons who were not conforming to wearing "gender-appropriate" clothing, and beat up others. Tired of the constant persecution, members of the community banded together to protect themselves against police violence. The response to police was famously termed "The Stonewall Riots," launching a bold new era of LGBTQ+ activism and advocacy.

181 "Stonewall Riots," *History.com*, June 26, 2020.

182 Ibid.

183 Katie Walsh, "Review: A 72-year lesbian romance for the ages revealed in 'A Secret Love'," *LA Times,* May 1, 2020.

184 "Stonewall Riots," *History.com*, June 26, 2020.

An important note about the Stonewall Riots: often erased from history books as early as the Stonewall uprising (incorrectly credited to gay and lesbian leaders when those who propelled the uprising were transgender women of color), transgender people—particularly transgender women of color—have continued to elevate LGBTQ+ voices and advocate on behalf of particularly low-income members of the community.[185]

Another advocacy area in which transgender women of color have been very vocal about is that of protecting sex workers and others in the informal economy. Because of lack of access to other economic opportunities and education, many trans women find that sex work is their only option of making an income.[186] According to a 2012 report from the National Transgender Discrimination Survey, 16 percent of the 6,400 trans adults surveyed reported resorting to sex work and selling drugs as a way to make ends meet.[187]

Indeed, transgender women of color have not only been on the forefront of activism and advocacy, but also the members of the LGBTQ+ community most subject to violence. According to a report conducted by the think tank *CityLab*, at least twenty trans or gender nonconforming women of

---

185 Christina Maxouris, "Marsha P. Johnson, a black transgender woman, was a central figure in the gay liberation movement," *CNN*, June 26, 2019.
186 U.S. Centers for Disease Control and Prevention, "Sex Workers," August 2016.
187 Jaime Grant, Lisa Mottet, Justin Tanis, Jack Harrison, Jody Herman, and Mara Keisling, "Injustice at Every Turn: A Report of the National Transgender Discrimination Survey," *National Center for Transgender Equality*, September 2012.

color were murdered in November 2019 alone.[188] Racism and transmisogyny—hatred of trans women—intersect in dangerous ways, allowing for these women to be killed without recompense.

Since the Stonewall Riots, the LGBTQ+ community has continued to create communities in neighborhoods of major cities, including the Castro District of San Francisco and the West Village in New York City. Much of the LGBTQ+ community's activism was centered around health care with the outbreak of the HIV/AIDS crisis. When a strange disease began afflicting predominantly young, healthy gay men across the United States, this caused chaos among the LGBTQ+ community. Quickly, young men were presenting in hospitals with fever, extreme fatigue, and pneumonia, among other symptoms, only to lose their lives weeks later.[189] Young people kept dying with little recognition and support from the federal government. In fact, by the time President Ronald Reagan said the word "AIDS" in public in 1985, over five thousand people had died from the disease.[190]

Government inaction, along with rhetoric from conservatives suggesting that those who had HIV were to be blamed, resulted in a groundswell of community organizing and support in the LGBTQ+ community.[191]

---

188 Ananya Garg, "What Cities Are Doing to Help Trans Women of Color," *CityLab*, February 27, 2020.

189 U.S. Centers for Disease Control and Prevention. "About HIV," July 14, 2020.

190 Richard Lawson, "The Reagan administration's unearthed response to the AIDS crisis is chilling," *Vanity Fair*, December 1, 2015.

191 Tim Fitzsimmons, "LGBTQ History Month: The early days of America's AIDS crisis," *NBC*, October 15, 2018.

Larry Kramer was one such advocate in the community.

***

While Larry Kramer passed away in May 2020 and was recently remembered as an elderly man of more than eighty years in poor health, he was a towering figure in LGBTQ+ and HIV/AIDS activism in the 1980s.[192] After Kramer's unhappy childhood living outside of Washington, DC, and graduation from Yale, he quickly moved to New York City, just in time to participate in the sexual revolution of the 1960s and 1970s.

His day job as a mail carrier allowed him time to write screenplays, where he gained even more income. His anger with a lover who did not want a monogamous relationship resulted in his explosive book, *Faggots*, which characterized the gay community as only taking pleasure from hedonistic sexual activity.

But when the AIDS pandemic came along, Kramer started realizing its impact on the community. In an interview with *The New York Times*, Kramer said, "In the Village, you couldn't walk down the street without running into some-body who said: 'Have you heard about so and so? He just died.' Sometimes you could learn about three or four people just walking the dog. I started making a list of how many people I knew, and it was hundreds. People don't comprehend that."[193]

---

192 John Leland, "Twilight of a Difficult Man: Larry Kramer and the Birth of AIDS Activism," *The New York Times,* May 19, 2017.

193 Ibid.

Having made enough money from screenwriting, Kramer focused his efforts on activism full-time, resulting in the establishment of the Gay Men's Health Crisis (GMHC), founded in his apartment in the New York neighborhood of Greenwich Village.[194] After some disagreement with fellow cofounders, Kramer went onto to establish the AIDS Coalition to Unleash Power (also known as ACT UP).[195]

GMHC provided volunteers to support the needs of those living with AIDS, including those who contracted the disease through intravenous drug use, through activities such as grocery shopping and spending time together.[196] More broadly, they also ran therapy groups for AIDS patients and their families and sent experts to speak at hospitals, church groups, and schools to dispel any misinformation about the gay community or the disease. Eventually, the federal government began responding by providing funding for research and educating the public on HIV/AIDS transmission. However, those early years of inaction continue to be seared into the minds of members of the LGBTQ+ community.

Since those early years of the HIV/AIDS epidemic, accessible health care remains an area of advocacy for the LGBTQ+ community. Whether because of insurance covering hormone treatments, gender affirming surgeries, or access to PrEP (an anti-retroviral drug that prevents the development of HIV), health care continues to be a challenge.

---

194 "GMHC: End AIDS. Live Life," *Gay Men's Health Crisis* website.

195 "ACT UP," *ACT UP* website.

196 Maureen Dowd, "For Victims of AIDS, Support in a Lonely Siege," *The New York Times,* December 5, 1983.

While this artwork came from a six-person art collective, it was created in response to the AIDS crisis and used as central image in ACT UP's campaign to raise awareness around the epidemic.[197]
Source: Wikipedia

---

197 for the image: "A pink triangle against a black backdrop with the words 'Silence = Death' representing an advertisement for the Silence = Death Project used by permission by ACT-UP, The AIDS Coalition to Unleash Power. Colour lithograph, 1987," *Wellcome Collection.*

While the height of the AIDS pandemic is seared in the minds of all who read about it in history books, it is far from over. Even now, Black and Latine men who have sex with men are more at-risk to get HIV/AIDS. According to the Centers for Disease Control, the number of HIV diagnoses among gay and bisexual men between 2010 and 2017 have significantly increased in Asian, Native American, and Native Hawaiian/ Pacific Islander populations.

HIV Diagnoses Among Gay and Bisexual Men in the 50 States and District of Columbia, 2010-2017[d]

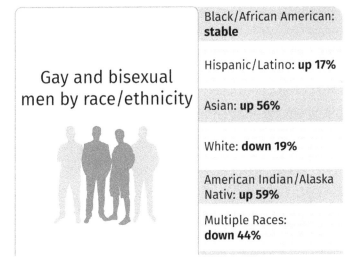

Source: Centers for Disease Control[198]

198 U.S. Centers for Disease Control. "HIV: Gay and Bisexual Men."

According to a 2017 Human Rights Watch report, members of the LGBTQ+ community are already at higher risk for psychological distress, drinking and smoking, and having multiple chronic conditions.[199] Transgender people in particular are more likely to be overweight, depressed, and have cognitive difficulties compared to cisgender people. These risks may be in part due to "minority stress," which is described as the added stress individuals face because they belong to a stigmatized group.

There has also been extensive research done in this community among youth as well. According to a paper published by open-access journal *Cureus*, LGBTQ+ youth are more likely to engage in high-risk sexual behaviors, leading to a higher incidence of sexually transmitted diseases (STDs).[200] Some of the root causes of these behaviors come from lack of education on safe sex practices and testing, and perception of STDs acquisition. If youth are able to access comprehensive sex education, it is typically taught through the lens of a heterosexual sexual encounter, thereby not centering the needs of LGBTQ+ youth in the process.

Moreover, because of their gender identities and/or sexual orientation, LGBTQ+ youth are more likely to be on the receiving end of bullying and peer victimization. According to a 2016 report published by the Gay, Lesbian, and Straight

199 "You Don't Want Second Best: Anti-LGBT Discrimination in US Health Care," *Human Rights Watch*, 2018.

200 Hudaisa Hafeeez, Muhammad Zeshan, Muhammad A. Tahir, Nusrat Jahan, and Sadiq Naveed, "Health Care Disparities Among Lesbian, Gay, Bisexual, and Transgender Youth: A Literature Review," *Cureus* 9, no. 4 (2017): 1-7.

Education Network (GLSEN), 25.5 percent of surveyed students reported hearing school staff make negative remarks about their gender expression.[201]

Perhaps even more telling, 73.9 percent of surveyed students reported personally experiencing some level of peer victimization, including verbal harassment, physical harassment, and cyberbullying. These behaviors result in negative mental health outcomes for LGBTQ+ youth.

Particularly for youth who are dependent on their parents' health insurance to access care, it can be even more challenging to get the care that they need. In homes where discussions about mental and sexual health are considered especially taboo, knowing that those services will be listed on a bill seen by parents increases not only barriers to access, but the fear of even trying.

Health insurance status is a critical part of anyone's health care experience, regardless of sexual orientation. But in the case of trans people seeking gender-affirming surgery—in which a person undergoes surgery to change sexual characteristics that better reflect that person's gender identity—accessing care can be a matter of life or death, especially from a mental health standpoint.

***

---

201 Emily Greytak, Joseph G. Kosciw, Christian Villenas, and Noreen M. Giga, "From Teasing to Torment: School Climate Revisited," *GLSEN*, 2016.

The LGBTQ+ community has long faced access problems with health care. While some of those are tied to issues of income and insurance, some access problems are further exacerbated by ignorance and bias. Some examples include health care providers being uncomfortable with seeing a patient because of their sexual orientation. While anecdotal evidence abounds, according to a national survey from the Center for American Progress in 2017, 8 percent of lesbian, gay, and bisexual people and 29 percent of transgender people reported a health care provider refused to see them because of their sexual orientation and gender identity.[202] This may be further reinforced if the health care organization chooses not to treat LGBTQ+ patients on religious grounds.

Carter (pseudonym), a twenty-five-year-old computer science doctoral student at the University of California, Berkeley, identifies as a trans man and shares how fundamental insurance status was as he went through gender affirmation surgery. When speaking about his own transition and gender affirmation surgery process, he stated he was able to take advantage of the comprehensive health insurance afforded to him through the guaranteed PhD funding package. He also shared:

> *"I was able to start hormones within a couple of months, and while I originally had to pay for them, they were free. I was also able to get a letter for top surgery from a psychiatrist after four sessions. I had the procedure done within a year for an amount within my price range."*

---

202 "You Don't Want Second Best: Anti-LGBT Discrimination in US Health Care," *Human Rights Watch*, 2018.

Seeing that insurance covered hormone therapy and surgery, Carter was able to go through the process with minimal financial burden. He also underscored the need for strong social support, sharing that he had a friend take him to the hospital.

These social connections that support queer community members in daily life and moments of crisis is known as "chosen family."[203] This term originated within the LGBTQ+ community and recognizes that a "chosen family" supports individuals especially when their biological families do not meet those emotional needs.

Carter emphasizes that, especially when going through intensive surgeries, having a "chosen family" to take care of you as you recover is critical. If you come from lower socioeconomic circumstance it's harder to, in Carter's words, "have someone who has time/money to care for you after a procedure (such as surgery)."

Carter pointed out the other inevitabilities of being a lower-income member of the LGBTQ+ community, stating:

"If you have a low level of security and/or socioeconomic stability, then you are less likely to be able to move your residency to an LGBTQ-friendly neighborhood that provides relevant services and to be insured, which is basically imperative to afford surgery costs."

---

203 Jeremy Nobel, "Finding Connection Through 'Chosen Family,'" *Psychology Today,* June 14, 2019.

The LGBTQ+-friendly neighborhood guarantees, to a certain extent, that "chosen family" is in close proximity. Connecting that statement to his own experience, Carter shared, "I was fortunate to be in a community where being trans is generally accepted, at a school where trans health care is relatively good." This made a world of difference for Carter; along with having strong social support through friendship, he also lived in a more tolerant neighborhood in Berkeley. In some ways, for low-income LGBTQ+ individuals who are located in less LGBTQ+-friendly areas, accessing culturally competent, sensitive care is not always possible.

Carter also pointed out other examples of miseducation and misconceptions associated with LGBTQ+ health, including seeing birth-assigned men who have sex with men (commonly known as MSM) not being allowed to donate blood; this also includes trans women.[204] Although these restrictions have been relaxed in the wake of the COVID-19 pandemic, there is contention indicating that this rule is left over from a bygone area of the beginning days of the HIV pandemic in the 1980s.

Miseducation abounds in regard to children and schools, as well. Gender nonconforming children are often not given access to medical treatments like puberty blockers and hormones, often with the justification that children's brains are not fully formed and so they cannot make their own decisions. However, some research from the University of

---

204 Maggie Shaw, "FDA's Revised Blood Donation Guidance for Gay Men Still Courts Controversy," *American Journal of Managed Care*, April 4, 2020.

Washington indicates that children who choose to transition, for example, already have a strong sense of identity.[205]

Moreover, in public schools, sex education is centered on a heterosexual experience. For example, high school students are most often taught that men should wear condoms during sexual intercourse, which has resulted in male condoms being made widely available on college campuses and at drugstores. However, cisgender lesbian women are not presented with as many options, which, according to Carter, may allow "many couples [to] assume in the moment no protection is necessary." Women should be educated in the suite of products that are designed for them, regardless of how their sexual partner identifies.

Carter also recognizes the education gap that might exist in medical/nursing school when it comes to caring for LGBTQ+, and especially trans, patients. While training on communicating with LGBTQ+ patients and recognizing implicit biases may not be standardized across clinical schooling, Carter emphasizes the use of resources such as the LGBT Health Education Implicit Bias Guide as a start.[206]

***

Carter's experience is not unique; trans people in the United States have an incredibly difficult time accessing health care.

---

205 Ed Yong, "Young Trans Children Know Who They Are," *The Atlantic*, January 15, 2019.

206 National LGBT Health Education Center, "Learning to Address Implicit Bias Towards LGBTQ Patients: Case Scenarios," September 2018.

Whether it's an annual checkup or an appointment to see a provider about a heart problem, the inherent mistrust of the medical system—and the psychological stress of having to constantly explain identity—is not unfamiliar to members of the trans community.

It certainly wasn't unfamiliar to Harvard Business School master's student Soltan Bryce.

Bryce, who has worked in health care for seven years, related his experience accessing gender-affirming care and hormone therapy (HRT) and its consequences. He shared the extent to which he has tried to protect himself through paperwork: "I've medically transitioned, so to speak. I've legally transitioned. I've even gone so far as to change my birth certificate."

Especially in light of the June 2020 ruling from the Trump administration that transgender health protections under the ACA were being reversed, Bryce highlighted how these policy actions further exacerbated the mistrust and fear members of the trans community experience when going to a health care provider.[207]

> "When you're trans, there's several parts of the journey. Not everyone does it the same way, but if you choose to change your name or your gender markers, it's a really vulnerable moment that you go through where maybe how you appear is really different than what you're called or how people perceive you. I think it's

---

207 Selena Simmons-Duffin, "Transgender Health Protections Reversed By Trump Administration," *NPR,* June 12, 2020.

really hard to summarize that experience of being courageous enough and bold enough to live in your true identity but to then have your past brought up in a way or being met with misunderstanding fear, or even worse, violence or harassment... it's just feels like a double whammy in the sense that it's already super vulnerable and then to be knocked down when you're already vulnerable is, I think, very hard."

Mistrust in the medical system, at least in terms of interpersonal interactions, is not specific to the trans community. But what is clear is the way that technology can make health care experiences difficult—in some cases, to the point of being traumatic—for trans people. The example that Bryce provided was the requirement of electronic health records (EHRs) to capture sexual orientation and gender identity data.

However, there has been massive confusion about how to capture it and where to put it on a billing form, especially in ways that accommodate the preferences of providers and payers. This can sometimes result in incorrect billing—which affects many Americans—but can be acutely hurtful to members of the trans community who may not get a bill paid by the insurer because of miscommunication about preferred name, for example.

According to Bryce, "There's this confusion at the systemic level. And if you think about the people whose lives are involved in that—what that means is every single technical detail that comes is because there's some kind of mismatch or problem in the way information is submitted or captured ...

If you don't fit into the format that is already designed, it becomes incredibly traumatic."

Bryce was kind enough to share more details about his experience transitioning while working for a health care company in DC. Here, in and of itself, Bryce was quick to point out that he would not have been able to transition before coming to DC, because the gender-affirming, surgery-providing, hormone therapy-providing physicians were highly concentrated in urban centers like DC, New York, and San Francisco among others. It is also important to point out that Bryce had health insurance through his employment with the company.

When he went to the general manager (GM) of the business, he was incredibly nervous and scared. Bryce mentioned leading with his vulnerability because he recognized that he needed help. The GM of the business, who was a high-level executive in the company, was not only very validating but also did a lot to support Bryce. "He helped me speak to some HR people who were incredibly accommodating. I don't even know the behind the scenes, but they just sort of made the surgery possible for me through our insurance...The HR person and GM really created a bit of a safety net around me."

While Bryce is keenly familiar with the challenges of the trans community with health care access because of personal experience, he was quick to point out the critical importance of getting the right support at the right time. As a young Palestinian refugee arriving to rural North Carolina with his family, Bryce noted, "The first healthcare we received in the United States was from the Red Cross."[208] Although America has huge, fundamental flaws, interacting with the Red Cross helped him understand America and make him a proud American.

This foundational experience led Bryce to develop a philosophy around how to create opportunities for others. In his words, "There's these opportunities [in the United States] to be the kind of person, the kind of organization, the kind of member of society that focused on creating opportunities for others. And creating opportunities for others becomes what happens when you provide the right support at the right time."

For Bryce, that means being a part of trans Facebook groups, WhatsApp chats, and spreading the word about Plume Health, a start-up for which he serves as head of growth. Plume Health seeks to bridge the gap between trans people looking to find gender-affirming care and hormone therapy (HRT) and gender-affirming providers.

And for Bryce, that's a start.

***

Carter stressed what many in the public health community believe. In Carter's eyes, "universal health care reduces one major barrier, which is getting insurance in the first place." Access to medical procedures and treatment should be

---

208 Harvard Business School, "Perspectives: Soltan Bryce, MBA 2021."

treated as a core right. Bryce would agree, stating that "So much of what our US health care system is designed to do is to tell us that employment equals insurance equals care… as we see in COVID times, when that chain breaks, a lot of bad things can happen."

Unfortunately, for trans people, these medical procedures are not considered "necessary," often touted as a desire that shouldn't be taken seriously. Specifically, for trans people, Bryce pointed out, "Even if there's access to care, the competency around gender-affirming care can be a problem. There's often times gatekeeping or long wait times, or just a lot of hoops to jump through to get care."

For example, a bitter custody dispute ensued between two parents in Texas in disagreement about how to handle their seven-year old child's identity exploration.[209] Senator Ted Cruz from Texas weighed in on this issue by stating he did not believe the child identifies as a girl and did not want the child to receive medical treatment to transition, even though that is what the child wanted.[210] According to Carter, this was incredibly insulting to trans people. Put simply, "it's not a want or feeling. It is a basic need."

There has been so much done in the past for LGBTQ+ health. Community pillars like Sylvia Rivera and Larry Kramer continued to fight for proper access to care and social services

---

209 Karen Zraick, "Texas Father Says 7-Year Old Isn't Transgender, Igniting a Politicized Outcry," *The New York Times,* October 28, 2019.

210 Jeremy Peters, "A Conservative Push to Make Trans Kids and School Sports the Next Battleground in the Culture War," *The New York Times,* August 18, 2020.

for LGBTQ+ health, ensuring housing and support for HIV/AIDS treatment and prevention. Individuals like Carter demonstrate the importance of insurance coverage in receiving gender-affirming care. Most importantly, people like Soltan Bryce and organizations like Plume make the path forward clear: leveraging technology to provide gender-competent care with compassion. The past, present, and future of the LGBTQ+ community's access to health care continues to drive the community to continue organizing and supporting each other's ability to do so.

PART FIVE

HEALING THE SLIGHTS

CHAPTER 9

BEYOND BUZZWORDS: LEVERAGING TECH TO INCREASE HEALTH CARE ACCESS

"Information is the lifeblood of medicine and health information technology is destined to be the circulatory system for that information."

—DR. DAVID BLUMENTHAL, PRESIDENT OF RESEARCH ORGANIZATION THE COMMONWEALTH FUND

It seems easy—perhaps a little too easy—to be enamored by all of technology's possibilities. Not long ago, seeking information was a chore only for those with money to buy the latest books or the time to peruse libraries and archives. Now, it seems every question can be answered in a matter of seconds. Perhaps more importantly, our society has rapidly transformed around the growth of technology use in our daily lives. Whether it's ordering a pizza, trading stock, or staying in touch with distant relatives, we have been able to harness the power of technology to make our lives more efficient.

What about in health care?

Many in health care are skeptical about using technology as a tool for change.

The first burn came from having to implement electronic health record (EHR) systems in hospitals and health systems. Health systems invest millions of dollars and countless hours to "go live" on and implement these EHRs. Meanwhile, clinicians' regularly having to navigate and input patient information into the system increases administrative burden and decreases the quality of time spent with their patients.

Dr. Atul Gawande of *Being Mortal* wrote about his experience being onboarded to Epic, one of America's largest electronic health record companies, as a Boston-based physician.[211] Stories of lengthened physician workdays and thousands of tech request tickets submitted to Epic abounded. This sort of technology implementation seemed burdensome and pointless, especially to medical providers primarily responsible for patient care.

Another topic—relying on technology as a panacea—dominated common conversation. Deploying technology in other industries—public or private—can have disastrous results.

---

211 Atul Gawande, "Why Doctors Hate Their Computers," *The New Yorker*, November 5, 2018.

Most notably, with the rise of computer-based risk assessments using supposedly objective measures to determine who is more likely to commit a future crime, someone Black has a higher likelihood of being rated as higher risk. Take the example that ProPublica presents in a 2016 article: Brisha Borden, a Black woman, was given the score of eight after she and a friend took a child's bike and scooter that were sitting outside.[212] Vernon Prater, a white man, who had an extensive crime record of armed robbery, was given a score of three after shoplifting from Home Depot.

It is critical for us to think about what this could mean for leveraging technology to improve care for marginalized communities. After all, algorithms and other technology-based automated systems are created by people who are bound to infuse their code with some level of bias and prejudice.

However, technology can be so much more than this. One of its positives, according to full-stack developer Byron Zhang, is that it can "automate things to reduce cost and free up resources to tackle other projects." And it can be used to mitigate the health disparities we've been seeing among vulnerable communities.

"Where mental health was five years ago is where social determinants of health are now."

---

212 Julia Angwin, Jeff Larson, Surya Mattu, and Lauren Kirchnere, "Machine Bias," *ProPublica,* May 23, 2016.

Something clicked when I heard this. Five years ago, people weren't openly discussing a new strategy their therapists recommended to set boundaries. People weren't talking about how their clinical depression was the actual reason they couldn't make it to happy hour. People weren't admitting to the burnout that they were experiencing at work, which was driving down their performance. Moreover, we've been seeing the increasing use of technology in the mental health space as more counseling occurs online (especially in light of the COVID-19 pandemic).

Companies like BetterHelp—which delivers online counseling—and Headspace—a meditation and mental wellness app—operate on the premise that mental health should be easily accessible at all times. It is essential to note that companies like BetterHelp have come under fire for their aggressive advertising strategies and lack of guarantee that users will speak to licensed professionals.[213] These types of criticisms are also indicative of the limitations of technology—for mental health in particular.

Mental health is not the only place where technology has been making strides. Recently, the social determinants of health have become a hot topic. In five years, people will start to talk more broadly about food access, safe neighborhoods that allow for exercise and fresh air, and stable housing that isn't near polluted areas as critical elements of health. They'll be thinking critically about how to use technology to improve circumstances and access to services.

---

213 Julia Alexander, "YouTube's BetterHelp mental health controversy, explained," *Polygon*, October 4, 2018.

And it'll be because of work that companies like Healthify are doing.[214]

***

Approximately seven years ago, a group of undergraduate students who were interested in addressing structural social barriers that people had with respect to accessing health care met up in a dorm room at Johns Hopkins University. One of the founders, Manik Bhat, was working at Harriet Lane Clinic as a volunteer through Health Leads, a volunteer program that believes in the power of holistic health management.

Bhat noticed Health Leads was very dependent on human capital but was not necessarily leveraging technology. Bhat recognized the absurdity of the fact that if he wanted to get pizza within a five-mile radius, it would be easy to find online, but for a low-income family searching for a food bank, that same technology was not available.

During an interview with Regional Vice President of Sales Bobby Murphy, Murphy described the goal of Healthify through this context: "Ultimately the underlying goal that Manik [Bhat] had was, let's create the infrastructure to allow social services to sit within the health care ecosystem, because today they do not."

---

214 "Who is Healthify?" *Healthify* website.

Incorporating social services is of utmost importance to health care outcomes, because we know now that social determinants of health drives up to 80 percent of health outcomes.[215] In this context, social service organizations are described as organizations that provide social supports to their clients, such as food, transportation, job training, and education, among other things.

The way that Healthify seeks to champion social services in the health care space is to create community referral networks, where community-based organizations can use a common platform to send and receive referrals to each other. Healthify contracts with these community-based organizations that are directly given patients' protected health information they are sharing. The key connector between big health systems, large health plans, and social service organizations of any size, however, is the convener stakeholder. These are typically organizations that financially back social service organizations, like United Way or Robert Wood Johnson Foundation. Conveners are incredibly important because while they are not directly providing services, they are aware of the cultural needs of their clients.

Once conveners and social service organizations are on Healthify's platform, the last step is to invite health plans and health systems that operate in a community to buy access to the conveners-social services organizations platform. This, said Murphy, is important for two reasons: "One, it creates

215 HMS Health Ideas Staff," Social Determinants of Health: The Impact on Members, Health Outcomes, and the Bottom Line," *Modern Healthcare,* March 6, 2019.

financial sustainability for the network because social services organizations are getting access to the platform, analytics, and reporting for free. [The network] doesn't have to be grant funded and it doesn't have to be funded by the foundation."

The second thing it does is sharpen the value proposition of social services organizations. Healthify is able to articulate the value of social services to health plans, which can direct the health plans to reimburse social services organizations for the services they provide. This, again, creates another form of financial sustainability for social services organizations that otherwise typically operate with small staffs and shoestring budgets. Given that in this model, social services organizations can rely on health plans to reimburse them directly, they are no longer strictly reliant on grants and donations to fund their service delivery. In the long term, this helps increase their capacity, and, most importantly, their ability to serve their communities.

Murphy also describes Healthify's work as constantly iterating. As evidenced by the chart below, on one side are the beneficiaries, or the patients who access the health systems, health plans, and social services organizations. On the other side are the policymakers who make key decisions on issues of health care access, quality, and cost. Healthify exists in the middle. Alongside health plans, health systems, and social service organizations, Healthify is able to continuously connect these institutions and share those learnings with policymakers to influence policy development and implementation. These stakeholders are then able to collaborate and iterate as needs of the populations they're serving continue to shift.

This allows for, for lack of a better term, an iterative cycle of innovation.

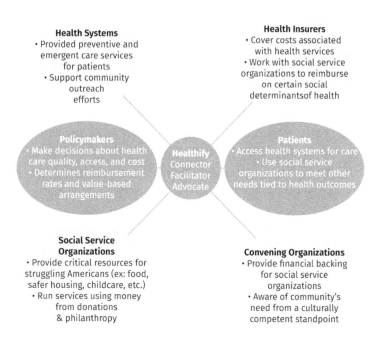

Most importantly, that innovation gets communicated to the stakeholders who have substantial influence on resource appropriations and policy function: policymakers. Healthify recognizes it cannot do this critical health care access work alone. In order to truly meet the needs of communities, Healthify seeks to leverage existing relationships between health systems and social services organizations to ensure the referral network they create through their platform benefits all involved.

But Healthify is not done yet. According to Murphy, they're seeking to grow more relationships, including with city and state agencies that oversee public health initiatives in various communities. What Healthify is doing is trying to better integrate all social services—including health care. After all, health care does not occur on its own, by itself, in a vacuum.

Through organizations like Healthify, the conversation around social determinants of health is moving beyond just a conversation. It's moving to action.

**

For some entrepreneurs, absurdity can be the mother of invention, as it was for Manik Bhat. But for Erica Jain, her entrepreneurship journey was personal.

Jain watched her mother struggle with weight loss for twenty-five years. Not until her mother obtained nutritional care through Jain's father's insurance was she able to stabilize her weight loss and live a consistently healthier life. Jain did further research and found a shocking statistic: while 85 percent of people who work with a nutrition professional reach a tangible health outcome, fewer than 5 percent actually have access to this type of care.[216]

In an interview, Jain indicated how deeply personal this nutrition journey was for her and her family: "What happened was, they [Jain's parents] started thinking differently.

---

216 "Healthie's Mission," *Healthie.com* website.

They started making different food choices and they started making tradeoffs of what they should eat." After working with a dietician, Jain's mother lost thirty-five pounds and kept it off for five years.

And that has made all the difference.

Jain has an extensive background in public health; after stints with Boston Consulting Group and the Clinton Health Access Initiative, she took matters into her own hands and founded Healthie,[217] a novel start-up that develops relationships between nutritionists, dieticians, and health systems to support better health outcomes for patients. According to Jain, "Traditionally, the health care system is not really designed to facilitate those long-term relationships so it's nice to have more of that coaching accountability and long-term view of a client's record."

Healthie functions as both practice management and telehealth platforms, allowing nutritionists to help patients log information about food consumption, schedule appointments, and take care of billing. Prior to Healthie's entry in the market, most nutritionists were cobbling together multiple tools that weren't designed for them. Jain mentioned most nutritionists "either are not using technology or are using technologies that aren't interoperable," resulting in a highly disjointed, fragmented communication system with the patient. Healthie allows nutritionists to have logistical challenges quickly taken care of so they can practice "top of license," a term that means practitioners can do more of

217 Ibid.

what they have studied to do. A common theme in health care is how fractured the overall ecosystem is; Healthie's value proposition is to bring different facets of patient care together.

To better serve marginalized communities, Healthie offers discounts to nonprofit partners who support their patients' nutrition needs. "They're doing the hard part, which is reaching these communities in need," Jain said in an interview. "We really consider ourselves to be a technology platform, but what's super cool is that technology scales, and so by virtue of having a technology platform, more and more people are able to use it."

While recognizing that insurance coverage continues to be a major thorn in the path of achieving health care access, Jain pointed to a promising trend for those who are insured: "Prevention is a good thing to cover, and insurance companies are covering [those] benefits at an increasing rate."

When asked about whether gradual or radical change would be more effective, Jain made one point very clear:

> *"Unless you rebuild from scratch, everything that you do, every improvement is going to be so piecemeal compared to standardizing. I think the government has to take a much more active role for them to create any real transformation, because otherwise the incentive structures are not there."*

***

One of the key challenges in implementing radical transformation in the health care system in the United States is how rigid and established the current system already is. The way we treat patients, bill and collect for payment, and interact with insurance companies has stayed almost the same for the past seventy years. However, full-stack developer Byron Zhang has had experience working on implementing health care change in developing countries with nascent health care infrastructures. For example, in developing countries across East Africa, Southeast Asia, and Latin America, he was engaged in a project that funded surgeons through a bundled payment model and paid based on outcomes.

In developing countries, getting surgeries done and paid for is incredibly challenging given the extreme access and cost issues that most families face. So, Zhang and his team worked on building a surgery infrastructure by connecting surgery patients to a website that would track the patient journey and connect providers to funders/donors that would cover financial expenses and pay based on outcomes. To increase capacity, these technologies were also used with volunteer doctors who came to these countries to support capacity. According to Zhang, once funding for this project became more secure, it became, "We'll give you 100K to 150K a month to fund a certain number of patients. And it was also cool because we bundled our payments."

In this way, technology became the way for health care to be effectively delivered and supported, without any barriers coming from mindsets like "well, that's how the system works."

Zhang also talked about the power of community health workers and building technology alongside the community. In fact, even in selecting which health systems to work with, his team made sure to choose the ones that were trusted by local communities. Community health workers are often people who come from within the community who are willing to connect fellow community members to health care resources. They often have the trust of community members because they are one of their own and are champions for important health care projects—like the ones that Zhang and his team were delivering.

Moreover, especially in rural areas, Zhang pointed out some communities have "been marginalized by the government in the past, so they already don't really trust the healthcare system. So, in these cases, it's super important to have community health workers." While community health workers are somewhat utilized in the United States—a famous example of this is when community health workers provide social support for high-risk patients—they have not been as widespread because of licensing and other regulations issues.[218]

Community health workers are able to leverage technology to improve access to care in developing country contexts. By supplying smart phones to community health workers, they are able to measure the distance between a patient's home and the nearest hospital, communicate patient outcomes

218 Shreya Kangovi, Nandita Mitra, David Grande, Judith A. Long, and David A. Asch, "Evidence-Based Community Health Worker Program Addresses Unmet Social Needs And Generates Positive Return On Investment," *Health Affairs* 39, no. 2 (2020): 207-213.

through photos, and track patient progress through using phone applications.

While Zhang and his team were able to make all of this progress, he also indicated some of the challenges, especially when working with government health ministries. Similar to what Murphy described, Zhang stated that developing the right technology was an iterative process. However, "governments are used to working in what we call a waterfall approach, where they have a twenty-page specification," which comes at odds with technology's smaller-scale approach.

***

Telemedicine has often been touted as a panacea for increasing health care access, particularly among rural Americans and hourly wage earners. The former live too far away from health care facilities and specialists to make consistent trips, and the latter run the risk of losing income when visiting their doctor. While it sounds simple, there is much work to be done to ensure telemedicine can be truly accessible.

Despite the incredible promise that telemedicine has shown in increasing access, many barriers still remain. For example, doctors' offices that provide virtual services will conduct an eligibility check to ensure the patient coming in for treatment will be covered by insurance for their visit. In some instances, insurance companies may choose not to cover the patient. They may be approving the claims that are submitted, but still telling the patient that they may have to pay out of pocket for care. These small barriers multiply for individuals who are elderly or homebound, who live in rural areas far away from specialists, or who cannot afford to take the time off from work to make a doctor's appointment.

According to the Chief Operating Officer of Beam Health, Ranga Jayawardena, there are some easy places to start.[219]

> "The way I would describe [telemedicine] is it's not a cure-all, but it is absolutely the lowest hanging fruit."

Like Amazon, Beam Health wants to "basically have a platform where any doctors, any medical practice, or health system can list their services, their providers. And then, they can use our software to do video appointments with existing patients as well as new patients Beam Health would help them acquire." In this way, Beam Health seeks to create the largest distribution network in health care. The idea to create this platform occurred a few years prior to the COVID-19 pandemic, which has allowed for a dramatic increase in virtual care use.

Ranga Jayawardena also underscored wanting to leverage network effects as part of Beam Health's underlying value proposition. Network effects, in this context, means that every new physician using the platform increases the variety and supply of physicians [available for virtual appointments], which ultimately drives demand. Other companies have used

---

219 *Beam Health* website.

network effects too, Jayawardena pointed out—"Over time, that's what Amazon did to really revolutionize online retail. So did Uber, Facebook, LinkedIn; these are the companies that have leveraged network effects for a crazy amount of growth."

Along with building a strong platform for physicians and patients to connect, telemedicine can make it easier for people to seek preventive services. Jayawardena mentioned a Philadelphia-based physician he spoke with did a study that 52 percent of Americans who are diagnosed with atrial fibrillation are diagnosed after they have an episode. Atrial fibrillation and other such heart conditions disproportionately affect Black Americans compared to their white counterparts, so, in Jayawardena's words, "If you can make it a lot easier for a patient to get in front of a healthcare provider, that ultimately leads to better health outcomes, right? It ultimately could lead to a lower burden on the health care system."

Comparing Beam Health to a department store, Jayawardena pointed out the benefits of a platform like Beam Health.

"By bringing sellers [physicians] together in one space, they may have to lower their prices in order to stay competitive. But because they're in a location where there's increased demand and people do foot traffic and people are going there, it's still worth it for the seller, right? Ultimately, they get so much demand that it is worth having lower prices. This dynamic could become extremely, extremely valuable for patients that no one is really even thinking about."

And he's right.

***

In an earlier chapter, Harvard Business School student Soltan Bryce was profiled about his health care experience as a trans person. Bryce also serves as head of growth for start-up Plume, which connects trans people to health services that support gender-affirming care and hormone therapy (HRT).[220] In the age of COVID-19 and social distancing, telehealth is now more important than ever, as indicated by comments made by Jayawardena above. According to a 2018 article published in Health Affairs, telehealth can reduce health disparities by creating equal opportunity for marginalized groups to access health care.

Plume was originally cofounded by two physicians, Dr. Matthew Wetschler and Dr. Jerrica Kirkley. Dr. Wetschler had extensive experience in telehealth and in emergency room settings, recognizing the opportunity that existed to deliver equitable care to some of society's most vulnerable. Dr. Kirkley has been a leading voice in advocating for gender-affirming care for trans people, especially in federally qualified health care settings. Best friends from medical school at the University of North Carolina at Chapel Hill, they put their heads together to find a way to bring their expertise to meet the trans community's needs. They also both recognized the dearth of gender-affirming providers in the United States and sought to ensure trans people could have access to care when they need it.

---

220 *Plume* website.

Did not see a doctor when they needed to because of fear of being mistreated as a transgender person.

Reported having at least one negative experience related to being transgender with a health care provided

33%

23%

Source: Plume website[221]

Bryce highlighted this last point by noting where gender-affirming providers are typically located: in urban centers. Most of these spaces started off as LGBTQ+ clinics developed in response to the HIV/AIDS crisis, which devastated the gay community in the 1980s. In Washington, DC, there's Whitman Walker; New York has Callen Lorde; in Boston, there's Fenway Health; Philadelphia has the Mazzoni Center; and San Francisco has UCSF.

Planned Parenthood also provides gender-affirming care, but its existence continues to be threatened because of legislation seeking to defund the organization.[222] The most recent estimate of how many trans people live in the United States came from the Williams Institute at the University of California, Los Angeles, stating that about 1.4 million trans

221 "Why Plume?" Plume website, May 27, 2020.
222 Katie Rogers, "BREAKING: Planned Parenthood defunded from the Title X Program" *Planned Parenthood of Indiana and Kentucky Inc.*, August 19, 2019.

people lived in the United States in 2016.[223] If you are a trans person who doesn't live near or has access to any of these urban centers—or a Planned Parenthood—you may not be able to get the access you need.

As someone who has worked extensively in health care's revenue management model, Bryce indicated what was unique about Plume: its direct-to-consumer, membership model. To become a member of Plume, you pay a monthly fee of ninety-nine dollars, which includes lab draws and consultations. While Plume currently doesn't support the cost of medications or gender-affirming surgery, it works with members to find affordable alternatives and resources to access those services.

This model can be an effective tool at improving access to care, especially for something like hormone therapy, which is non-acute and requires chronic support. Bryce thought, "What if we're leveraging amazing technology to do it in this digital-first way where you don't have to leave your job to go get an appointment at a clinic an hour away; you can just literally, through using an app on your smartphone, text with your gender affirming care competent provider and get your HRT in the same day?" Given the challenges that trans people typically face in accessing gender-affirming care—including wait times and denials for surgery and therapy—this is revolutionary.

223 Andrew Flores, Jody Herman, Gary Gates, and Taylor Brown, "How Many Adults Identify as Transgender in the United States?" *UCLA School of Law Williams Institute*, June 2016.

What is incredibly unique about the Plume team is that at least half of Plume's providers and care coordinators identify as trans. Not only are they able to bring their clinical and administrative expertise to the table, many of them directly understand what their patients are going through and can counsel them accordingly.

Once you get the Plume membership, you have direct access to the care team to schedule video appointments for communication and prescription letters for hormone therapy. Plume partners with Quest Diagnostics for lab draws, which are covered in the subscription model. Plume handles calling in prescription orders to local pharmacies that patients can access, with the future goal of delivering medications directly to the patient's home.

Plume already has a lot to be proud of. In the span of six months, it has expanded its presence to ten states and currently covers 50 percent of the trans population in the United States. According to Bryce, Plume is poised to become the largest provider of HRT for the trans community. Other projects on the horizon include designing EHRs around the trans experience and becoming the largest aggregator of longitudinal data about the trans community.

Ultimately, Plume's goal is to provide trans people with the health care they deserve. Beyond focusing on care in the trans community, Bryce voiced additional goals, including "increasing the visibility and importance of gender affirming care. In our biggest, wildest dreams, we improve the health care of every trans life." To scale capacity, partnering with other providers and becoming a connector of care are other foreseeable goals for Plume.

Plume is the first time that Bryce has had a trans peer or colleague in the workplace. The team he works with continues to make him aware of the need to design systems—and technology—inclusively. According to Bryce, we should keep designing policies and systems while asking: "Who are we missing? Whose voices aren't heard?"

Because it can make all the difference.

***

From Murphy, we learned that technology can be a great coordinating tool to increase communication between health care stakeholders and build the financial capacity of social services organizations in charge of improving various social determinants of health. Jain's product, Healthie, helped us understand the value of technology to track progress and streamline processes. In the stories of his work outside of the United States, Zhang pointed to technology as an efficient way to gather information and build community trust. And here at home, Jayawardena and his team at Beam Health pointed out the large-scale impacts of bringing physicians and patients seeking virtual care together on the same platform.

When leveraged correctly and in coordination with other services, technology does not need to be an unwieldy, cumbersome tool to use at the exhortation of government agencies. It can also be used to change lives.

Not only is having sleek user interfaces and using technology to coordinate with other platforms critical but being able to engage with different stakeholders is as well. For example, Zhang pointed out that the only way to make some of the work his team did to scale surgery capacity was to be in concert with the government's desires to create interoperable and open-source technology.

Technology alone is not enough. Engaging with community stakeholders—particularly government and policymakers— is vital. In the United States in particular, the government spends billions of dollars on health care—whether through Medicare or Medicaid; outreach efforts in cities, towns, and states; or supporting the teaching work of academic medical centers. The government continues to be a critical stakeholder in the health care conversation.

Perhaps more importantly, the government makes decisions about which institutions to regulate and to what extent they should be regulated. It is clear that government in the United States—whether federal, regional, or local—has the power to design new policies, strengthen existing ones, or get rid of what is not working.

Understanding how to leverage existing policy is a great place to start.

CHAPTER 10

STANDING ON THE SHOULDERS OF GIANTS: HEALTH POLICY AS AN ENGINE FOR CHANGE

———

"America's health care system is neither healthy, caring, nor a system."
—WALTER CRONKITE, TELEVISION NEWS ANCHOR AND BROADCASTER

When thinking about creating transformational change in American society, two essential ingredients are necessary: shifting cultural narratives and shifting policy directions. The former is by far the most challenging, but it does not happen without the latter. Throughout the twentieth century, life-changing policies were passed by presidents that resulted in increased access to health care for the unemployed, the elderly, the disabled, and other vulnerable groups.

Starting with President Franklin Roosevelt, who had intended to make health care his next big crusade before his untimely death, onwards, health care policy has been on the minds of every president. President Harry Truman was soundly thwarted in his efforts to pass legislation supporting universal health care not once, but twice. As part of his "War on Poverty," Lyndon Johnson ensured the passage of seminal legislation supporting the development of health care infrastructure for the elderly through Medicare and the poor through Medicaid. Attempts to reform health care under the Clinton administration came under fire for removing patient choice; many recall the "Harry and Louise" advertisements that graced television sets in the evenings, portraying a middle-aged couple worried about what government-controlled health care would mean for their wallets and quality of life.[224]

The most recent—and perhaps most hotly debated—health care legislation has been the Affordable Care Act, passed during the Obama administration. Much of it—if not all of it—has been subject to debate in the past ten years.

But policy does not only occur at the federal level. State and local policies are often specifically written to cater to local populations and contexts. Within those contexts, people operate and access health care.

We often learn about policy within the context of civil rights, especially through Supreme Court cases. Brown v. Board

---

224 Dan Diamond, "Pulse Check: 'Harry and Louise'—and Hillary," *POLITICO,* May 12, 2016.

of Education (1954) overturned "separate but equal" provisions in public places established by Plessy v. Ferguson (1896). Loving v. Virginia (1967) upended anti-miscegenation laws, allowing Black and white people to marry.

But what about health care policy?

Some ways to innovate in the policy space include:

- Subverting existing policy to serve the needs of vulnerable populations
- Paying close attention to current health care trends and the rise of key health care players in devising policy
- Recognizing the history of health care policy in the United States—especially as it relates to universal health coverage—as we try to plan for a brighter future

I examine some of these examples below.

***

A tall, gangly physician with a crooked smile greets patients and administrators in San Francisco County's Department of Health Services with warmth and caring. This is Dr. Mitchell Katz, who, in 1991, served as the lead for this department. Guided by his own personal experience of having siblings with developmental disabilities, one of whom struggled with mental health and homelessness, Dr. Katz has made the poor and vulnerable the very center of the health programs he directs and has directed.[225] Dr. Katz has had extensive experience working in safety net hospital systems, ensuring that the most vulnerable in San Francisco have access to high-quality health care.

Why is supporting economically and socially vulnerable patients so critical? In the words of Dr. Katz's widely acclaimed TED Talk: "Health care is built on a middle-class model that often doesn't meet the needs of low income patients."[226] These patients suffer worse health outcomes not only because of their lack of access to quality health care, but also because of their inability to successfully access other social services.

Dr. Katz recognized this too, especially among more stigmatized conditions, and his results-proven career has a lot to show for it.

Arriving in San Francisco County in 1991, Dr. Katz quickly learned that AIDS was San Francisco County's number one cause of death, transmitted especially through needle sharing by intravenous drug users. Dr. Katz recognized the unique opportunity this presented to develop a needle exchange program. He also realized how controversial such a program would be.

225 Scott James, "A Life Devoted to Health, Framed by His Siblings' Disabilities," *The New York Times,* December 16, 2010.
226 Katz, Mitchell. "What the US healthcare system assumes about you." Filmed November 2018 in Palm Springs, CA. TEDMED video, 15:52.

At the time, needle exchange programs were considered enabling to those using intravenous drugs.[227] The thought of taxpayer money being used to "fund someone's drug habit" seemed almost unconscionable. To ensure a needle exchange program could be legally sponsored by San Francisco County's health department, Dr. Katz began researching California statutes that provide that kind of information.

He learned that one California statute in the Health and Safety Code, AB136, mandated that, by declaring a public health emergency, state law could temporarily be suspended. Specifically, this statute made official an interpretation of the California Emergency Services Act that would be used by local jurisdictions to approve syringe exchange programs throughout the state.[228]

This began a robust public health campaign to ensure that local government administrations would understand AIDS as a public health emergency. Several strategies were deployed to ensure local jurisdictions would support such programs, and San Francisco County felt comfortable declaring a public health emergency. Given the way AB136 was written, the declaration of a public health emergency had to be done every two weeks. Over a nine-year period, these declarations every two weeks allowed two million dirty needles to be exchanged for clean ones.

---

227 Emma Jacobs, "Needle Exchange Program Creates Black Market in Clean Syringes," *NPR*, January 3, 2015.

228 Ricky Bluthenthal, Keith Heinzerling, Rachel Anderson, Neil Flynn, and Alex Kral, "Approval of Syringe Exchange Programs in California: Results From a Local Approach to HIV Prevention," *American Journal of Public Health* 98, no. 2 (2008): 278-283.

San Francisco County became an example for at least four other counties in California. This novel needle exchange program motivated California to finally pass, in 2011, a needle exchange program that could be funded without an emergency order.

**

Another critical component of reducing health disparities is understanding people's relationships with each other. In the late 1990s, Dr. Katz and his team learned San Francisco County was suffering from staggering rates of chlamydia infection, but they were again stymied by state law. According to Katz, it was difficult to get people to bring in their partners.

Imagine this: You are a gynecologist treating a privately insured female patient for chlamydia. You write a prescription for your patient, only for her to return a few weeks later presenting the same symptoms. Upon further questioning, your patient at first feels embarrassed but, through tears, reveals that her male partner has not been treated for chlamydia, causing her to become reinfected. A pattern thus emerged: in heterosexual relationships, the woman would come in to receive treatment, but would likely be reinfected unless her male partner was also treated.

Quickly realizing that most male partners would be unwilling to come in to receive treatment, Dr. Katz sought best practices deployed by gynecologists treating privately insured patients. After learning those physicians would give a prescription to an infected partner for her partner or spouse, Dr. Katz sought to find legal alternatives that would allow his government doctors to provide this support without breaking the law. Again, Dr. Katz was successful in finding a section of the California Health & Safety Code that authorized county and local health officials to take "all necessary measures" to prevent the transmission of infectious diseases.

In 1998, by garnering county support politically, Dr. Katz was able to motivate shifts in the county policy, allowing doctors to prescribe medicines for the infected person's spouse/partner. Most importantly, Dr. Katz and his team conducted a telephone survey to understand the impact of physicians doing this on the sexual health of female patients and their male partners. While this survey gathered momentum, Dr. Katz also ensured that he was able to gather support from the state medical society to build appropriate consensus.

In 2005, a formal study was published that proved that providing medications for women's sexual partners helped prevent significant amounts of recurrent STDs.[229] By 2004, the number of syphilis cases, including repeat cases, dramatically reduced from 522 to 391 because of these new prescribing guidelines, community outreach, and patient education.

---

229 Jeffrey Klausner, Charlotte Kent, William Wong, Jacque McCright, and Mitchell Katz, "The Public Health Response to Epidemic Syphilis, San Francisco, 1999-2004," *Sexually Transmitted Diseases* 32, no. 10 (2005): S11-S18.

Syphilis Cases in San Francisco (1999-2004)

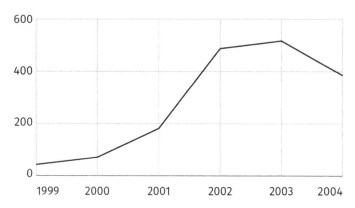

Source: This instrumental study proved Dr. Katz's policy effective in reducing syphilis cases in San Francisco.[230]

It is no surprise that based on his experience in California, Dr. Katz understands how to achieve better health care for vulnerable populations. By understanding what needs to be done and identifying creative ways to implement solutions, Dr. Katz has been successful in not only improving health outcomes, but also restoring dignity to these patient populations.

In his words, "no extra charge for that."

***

230 Bluthenthal, Ricky, Keith Heinzerling, Rachel Anderson, Neil Flynn, and Alex Kral, "Approval of Syringe Exchange Programs in California: Results From a Local Approach to HIV Prevention," *American Journal of Public Health* 98, no. 2 (2008): 278-283.

In the age of personalized technology and health care wearables, the one key challenge in health care that is undeniable is how one-size-fits-all health care remains.

At least that is what esteemed Health Care Speaker and Consultant Dr. Jon Burroughs believes.

Describing health care challenges in America, for Dr. Burroughs, is about understanding that it is not currently meeting people where they are. He compared our current health care system to the Ritz Carlton—there are very few of them, and they are very expensive. Unlike the hotel industry—which spans from establishments like the Ritz Carlton and The Four Seasons to the Fairfield Inn—health care provides the same model across the board.

"Now, the problem in health care in the twentieth century is we created a one size fits all," said Dr. Burroughs in an interview. "That means you either got a doctor or you got the emergency room, which is fine if you have money, but it's not fine if you're poor, or even lower middle class. So, we built a Ritz Carlton. And what we didn't do is create other brands within healthcare that were good enough."

At the end of the day, according to Dr. Burroughs, "We built a very monolithic healthcare system designed to take care of people who had cash."

While there may be minute differences based on the type of hospital (e.g., community health clinic, academic medical center, or large corporate health system), Dr. Burroughs' words still hold true. Health care is still one size fits all.

As we know, through countless news reports about surprise bills, discrimination based on pre-existing conditions, and continued bias against communities of color, this is not news.

However, according to Dr. Burroughs, there are some policy changes that are being leveraged. Fully recognizing some of these solutions are necessarily implemented at the state and local level because of constitutional purview, Dr. Burroughs outlines ways in which we can expand access to health for more economically vulnerable Americans. These include:

- Increasing the capacity of care provided by nurse practitioners and physician assistants
- Making the necessary investments in virtual care, recognizing its effectiveness
- >Paying attention to new entrants into the health care market, such as CVS, Walgreens, and Walmart, which are creating retail outlets for fairly inexpensive care
- Health care systems developing "ambulatory portfolios" that provide the consumer with choice about how much to pay and what kind of service they want to receive
- Using predictive and business analytics strategically to understand the socioeconomic circumstances of patients and the type of care they will need as a result
  - Large health care systems such as Intermountain Healthcare in Salt Lake City or Baylor Scott & White in Texas are using predictive analytics to do population-based health models. In this way, they are able to identify high-risk populations and service areas that will need more attention.

Dr. Burroughs also talked extensively about the ways in which the health care workforce is shifting, given how the health care system is now more focused on coordinated, integrated care.

"And the leader of the new health care team isn't going to be a physician, it's going to be a care coordinator or navigator," said Dr. Burroughs. "So, you're going to need care coordinators who have both a clinical background and a business background, and who truly understand the environment care and all the payers." Policies should support the empowerment of these now-emerging health care workforce members by building the right infrastructure around them. As such, there needs to be more empowerment and engagement with "people who have mastery of the [health care] system." According to Dr. Burroughs, this includes deep understanding of pharmacy benefits management (third party entities that administer prescription drug plans on behalf of health insurance companies), health care policy and regulatory affairs, and health law.[231]

Dr. Burroughs shared the inevitability of inequality manifesting in health care: "It's not going to be equal. And this is something Americans struggle with: people with money are going to always be able to pay for a higher level of service and a higher level of access. And that's never going away."

While recognizing this means those at the lower levels of the socioeconomic ladder will receive worse services, Dr.

---

231 "Pharmacy Benefit Managers and Their Role in Drug Spending," *The Commonwealth Fund,* April 22, 2019.

Burroughs highlighted, "If payers are smart to provide a good enough service that doesn't have a significant [negative] impact on the outcome or cost of care, that's the litmus test."

So, our policies need to do a better job creating tiers of health care services that are high quality for people at different levels of health and insurance status.

Our policies also need to do a better job supporting primary care providers who serve the communities they come from—who grew up on the streets in Harlem in New York City, who know the barbershops and hair salons that line the neighborhoods in Compton, and who comfortably chat with grocery store workers in their neighborhood in West Philadelphia. When these independent physicians are unable to financially survive in an increasingly consolidated market, it can create anticompetitive tendencies and reduce quality of care.[232] This, in turn, can negatively affect marginalized communities in improving health outcomes.

It begs the question: What are the policy solutions at play here?

**

SOMOS is an independent physician association (IPA) dedicated to providing primary care for Medicaid beneficiaries in vulnerable urban communities.[233] Based in New

---

232 Alex Kacik, "Monopolized healthcare market reduces quality, increases costs," *Modern Healthcare,* April 13, 2017.

233 *SOMOS* website.

York City, SOMOS is a network of nearly 2,500 providers across four boroughs—the Bronx, Queens, Manhattan, and Brooklyn—determined to address the health care needs of their communities by targeting social determinants of health. SOMOS is comprised of three community-based Physician IPAs—Corinthian, Excelsior, and Eastern Chinese American Physicians—and also works with several community-based organizations to address social determinants of health more directly.

What makes SOMOS so interesting is it leverages the collective strength of independent physicians to ensure it can negotiate for competitive rates. In a world slowly shifting to value-based care, SOMOS' current model allows the provider to take on more risk while allowing them to reap the benefits of providing high-quality preventive care for their patients. In this way, IPAs like SOMOS can maintain financial viability while also providing appropriate, culturally sensitive preventive care to its populations.

This is especially helpful in New York State given the Delivery System Reform Incentive Payment (DSRIP) program. DSRIP was originally designed to improve outcomes and reduce avoidable hospital use by 25 percent. It really behooves primary care providers to get involved in value-based payment arrangements, because otherwise the insurance companies end up having more outsized benefits.

As the only physician-led group to be designated as a Value-Based Payment Innovator by the State of New York, SOMOS continues to remain committed to providing culturally competent care while supporting physicians providing critical primary care services.[234]

In Spanish, *somos* means "we are." The impetus behind SOMOS is collaborative; the physicians work alongside community members to not only establish better health outcomes, but to be their true partners in their primary care journey.

Research continues to be done in the space of social determinants of health and how to improve them. Policies need to be more cognizant of the importance of predictive analytics, of coordinating social service systems, and of improving the provision of social services to vulnerable populations.

With Medicare for All on the horizon, does the policy space have what it takes to innovate?

***

The hot item on everyone's minds includes upcoming debates on Medicare for All legislation. Medicare for All has an older history than what you might think, dating back to when Medicare was first announced to provide health care coverage for the elderly in the mid 1960s. According to Professor Jonathan Oberlander of the University of North Carolina at Chapel Hill, "The original idea behind Medicare was

---

234 "Evolent Health and SOMOS IPA Aim to Provide Physician-Driven Medicaid Managed Care through New York Innovator Program," *CISION PR Newswire*, November 6, 2018.

Medicare for all."[235] The hope was lawmakers would incrementally expand Medicare to larger swathes of the population.

Except that never happened.

Years before, labor leaders put in a lot of effort to think critically and advocate for universal health coverage, but businesses and doctors—as well as the American Medical Association—quashed that plan quickly. When President Franklin D. Roosevelt wanted to add health coverage to the Social Security Act of 1935, the same forces tried to shut it down. The defeat that Truman suffered in the fight for universal coverage silenced any efforts to reform health care for at least the subsequent 20 years.[236] Lyndon B. Johnson came the closest to universal health care reform by providing federally subsidized health care for the elderly through Medicare and state-subsidized health care for the poor through Medicaid.

Reforms popped up in the 1970s, with efforts made by Democratic Senator Ted Kennedy to introduce a national health insurance plan (which failed) and Republican Senator Jacob Javits, who proposed expanding Medicare to cover the entire country's population. While the idea was not considered politically palatable enough to pass, Javits was quickly associated with the term "Medicare for All."[237]

Under the more conservative Reagan administration, activists began taking charge. While HIV/AIDS activists are the

---

235 Abigail Abrams, "The Surprising Origins of 'Medicare for All,'" *TIME*, May 30, 2019.

236 Ibid.

237 Ibid.

first to come to mind during this time period, groups such as Physicians for a National Health Program and the Gray Panthers emerged as advocates for meaningful health care reform. While they pushed for "single payer" health care, similar to what is seen in Canada, it didn't catch on outside of health policy and activist spaces. There was still great hesitation in explicitly mentioning "socialized medicine."

Health care reform under President Clinton, for this reason, inched away from "single payer," marking an important conservative shift in the Democratic approach to health care. Oberlander shared that Clinton's reform was focused on the fact that "the only feasible way to pass health care reform was one that built on the status quo and built on private insurance."

At the start of the twenty-first century, Americans were hankering for further innovation in the health policy space, pushing President George W. Bush to create Medicare Part D to cover the cost of prescription drugs. However, the inability of the federal government to negotiate these costs left progressives feeling bereft of making true progress.

The Affordable Care Act, passed in 2010 under the Obama administration, aimed to improve health care coverage by creating state and federally run marketplaces for those who were not receiving health care through employment. It also sought to increase insurance coverage through encouraging Medicaid expansion for the poor across states.

A study conducted by The Commonwealth Fund identifies that while the percentage of US adults who are inadequately insured hasn't changed, fewer adults are uninsured today, and the duration of coverage gaps people experience has significantly shortened.[238] This was further supported by the extensive literature review provided by Soni et. al, who found encouraging evidence of improvements in health outcomes, especially in chronic disease, neonatal and maternal health, and mortality, as a result of having health insurance coverage.[239] However, some criticism, including that stemming from current Center for Medicare and Medicaid Services administrator Seema Verma, points to Obamacare's "failure to deliver affordable insurance premiums and has created a new class of uninsured."[240]

Those on the left have also had contention with the ACA's reliance on private, for-profit insurers to fund health care. In a Harvard Public Health Review article penned by the founders of Physicians for a National Health Plan, the authors lamented that because of this reliance on private insurance, "insurers are finding ways to subvert these regulations, e.g. through tiered pharmacy benefits that discriminate against enrollees with potentially expensive illnesses such as HIV, Parkinson's, seizures, psychosis, and diabetes."[241]

---

238 Sara Collins, Herman Bhupal, and Michelle Doty, "Health Insurance Coverage Eight Years After the ACA," *The Commonwealth Fund*, February 7, 2019.

239 Aparna Soni, Laura Wherry, and Kosali Simon, "How Have ACA Insurance Expansions Affected Health Outcomes? Findings From The Literature," *Health Affairs* 39, no. 3 (2020).

240 Seema Verma, "Thank Obamacare for the Rise of the Uninsured," *CMS. gov*, September 13, 2019.

241 Dominic Caruso, David Himmelstein, Steffie Woolhandler, "Single-Payer Health Reform: A Step Toward Reducing Structural Racism in Health Care," *Harvard Public Health Review* no. 7 (2015): 1-4.

***

Half a century later, "Medicare for All" is a slogan we have heard time and time again, especially at the start of the race for the Democratic presidential nominee in 2019. Former presidential contender and well-known progressive Bernie Sanders first introduced Medicare for All as a bill in the House of Representatives a mere three years after the passage of the Affordable Care Act. While at that time no one would cosponsor with him, the 2019 version of the bill had fourteen cosponsors.

Medicare For All (at least, Bernie Sanders's version) has garnered massive support among the young and those in vulnerable communities. This has become increasingly true in the wake of the COVID-19 pandemic. According to global data intelligence company Morning Consult, support for Medicare For All has reached an all-time high at 55 percent of registered voters.[242] When looking at the demographic breakdown of Medicare for All supporters, support significantly increased among people in the $50,000-$100,000 income bracket, voters between forty-five and fifty-four years old, and Black voters.

While "socialized medicine" has become less stigmatized than it was in the past, there is still some lack of clarity around what "Medicare for All" truly means. Previous presidential contenders like South Bend mayor Pete Buttigieg supported efforts around "Medicare for all who want it,"

---

242 Yusra Murad, "As Coronavirus Surges, 'Medicare for All' Supports Hits 9-Month High," *Morning Consult,* April 1, 2020.

while current Democratic presidential nominee Joe Biden supported the idea of introducing a Medicare-like option alongside current private plans.

As has been made clear throughout the history of health reform in the United States, there is no one particular direction the country is committed to. Previous and current efforts to form a more nationalized, public approach to health care have been thwarted by lobbying groups and conservative politicians. This will prove to be even more challenging in the coming months, especially with the advent of the 2020 presidential election.

We have seen creative ways to leverage policy, such as how Dr. Mitchell Katz took advantage of local laws to ensure the success of a needle exchange program. He was also able to notice trends and patterns in how heterosexual women were receiving chlamydia treatment and ensure policies supported comprehensive, holistic care for those women and their male partners. Dr. Burroughs detailed other challenges in our health care system and the variety of solutions being brought up, including leveraging other clinicians and paying attention to new entrants in the health care market. Independent physicians' associations like SOMOS continue to meet patients where they are—in their homes, in their communities—reinforcing the power of culturally competent health care. All of these examples continue to remind us of the journey America has taken with health insurance and all the places this country is still planning—or not planning—to go.

What does this history of health reform indicate about the United States' philosophical approach to health care?

CHAPTER 11

LOOKING TO THE PAST TO UNDERSTAND OUR FUTURE: HEALTH CARE PHILOSOPHY IN THE UNITED STATES

———

"When a health policy analyst went to heaven, he asked God the same question: 'Will America ever have a single-payer system?' And God said, 'Absolutely. Just not in my lifetime.' I'm afraid that little story is true. Americans are just not prepared to let government be responsible for all of their healthcare."

—DR. STUART ALTMAN, ECONOMIST AND PROFESSOR AT BRANDEIS UNIVERSITY

Given the flurry of debate around universal health coverage in recent months, it begs the question: Why is one of the world's most powerful countries even having this conversation to begin with? Most comparable countries, like the United Kingdom and Canada, have some semblance of national health care coverage.

Around the same time President Truman was soundly defeated in his attempts to pass health care reform, the United Kingdom established the National Health Service (NHS) as part of its rebuilding efforts after World War II had decimated the former great colonial power.

The origin story of the NHS is what undergirds strong and sustained public trust. According to an interview with *CNN*, Director of Research and Chief Economist at the health think tank Nuffield Trust John Appleby said, "There's sort of a folk memory of it … people wanted a really big change and the NHS was part of it."[243]

A deep sense of collectivism was humming in the UK post-World War II, along with underlying values of the importance of health care being equal, fair, and free. Even the framing of the NHS still comes from a place of community.

Appleby stated, "Virtually everybody contributes to the NHS in some way, there is no special NHS tax, it is not just funded out of income tax, it is funded out of all taxes. So everybody is putting in something, and the deal is, no matter who you

---

243 Ivana Kottasová, "Britain's health service is part of its national psyche. It's also on life support," *CNN*, April 18, 2020.

are, whether you're the Queen or me, there's equal access to the things you need when you need them, and it's not decided on your income but on your healthcare needs."

The undergirding philosophy behind the NHS is that one shouldn't have to pull out their wallet to pay for an annual physical exam, a chemotherapy session, or the delivery of their child.

The NHS has seen its fair share of financial problems—like Medicare in the United States, there is a concern about ensuring the NHS is sufficiently funded to meet patient demand. While many in the country have stepped up to volunteer or donate money in times of crisis, there is a continued fear that the government will not invest in the NHS in the ways that it should.

The single payer health care system through which most Canadians receive health care is similarly troubled, but beloved. In the United States specifically, most Americans only hear about how Canadians have long wait times to access basic care. According to The Commonwealth Fund, 43 percent of Canadians reported that they were able to get a same-day or next-day appointment at their regular place of care when they needed medical attention.[244] Having established a single payer system in the 1966, despite its flaws, Canadians also seem to positively rate their health care experience. Federal legislation passed in 1966 pledged the cost of financing of provincial health care plans would be evenly

---

244 Milan Korcok, "Canada's single-payer healthcare system—a system in turbulence, but beloved nonetheless," *International Travel & Health Insurance Journal*, February 3, 2020.

shared by the provinces and federal government. According to an article in the *International Travel & Health Insurance Journal*, 94 percent of Canadians consider it a source of national pride.[245]

In post-apartheid South Africa, its constitution states that health care is a human right.

So why won't the United States say the same?

The most common moral and philosophical arguments are rooted in American exceptionalism, a more individualist mentality ("pulling yourself up by your bootstraps"), and deep mistrust in government and public institutions. Many still swear by Reagan's quote "The nine most terrifying words in the English language are: I'm from the government and I'm here to help."

But racism and discrimination have a role to play here as well.

***

A *New York Times* op-ed from March 2020—written just when stay-at-home orders started to hit certain states in the United States—boldly states that "racism has forever been a forbidding obstacle to the development of a welfare state, at least of the sort that Europe enjoys and many Americans aspire to."[246] In the United States in particular, racism con-

---

245 Ibid.
246 Eduardo Porter, "Why America Will Never Get Medicare for All," *The New York Times*, March 14, 2020.

tinues to feel incredibly pervasive—especially in the height of police brutality protests—but is also the elephant in the room.

The author of this op-ed is Economics Reporter Eduardo Porter, who outlines the ways in which people of color in the United States were left behind when opportunities to build wealth came along. Some of this, writes Porter, was the result of political jockeying that President Franklin Roosevelt had to do with Southern Democrats in the 1930s. In order to win their support, President Roosevelt had to lock out communities of color from New Deal policies that were responsible for expanding homeownership. As a result, white families were able to enjoy an unprecedented level of wealth and asset building compared to their Black peers. New Deal labor codes excluded those holding farm work and domestic jobs—both industries dominated by Black employees.

As referenced earlier in the chapter, President Johnson fought to overcome passing Medicare and Medicaid to provide care for the elderly and the poor. This is part of what makes President Johnson, according to historian Doris Kearns Goodwin, one of the most socially progressive presidents the United States has ever seen.[247] However, in obtaining the passage of this legislation—and the eventual desegregation of health care facilities—the delicate balance between Southern and liberal Democrats began to fray.

---

247 Robert Kuttner, "A Conversation with Doris Kearns Goodwin," *The American Prospect,* December 17, 2007.

President Nixon promised to be tough on crime, while squarely pointing a finger at the Black community. According to notes in the diary of his chief of staff, he said, "The key is to devise a system that recognizes this [Black people being a "problem"] while not appearing to." This led to the development of mass incarceration, which disproportionately affected—and continues to affect—Black people.

The Reagan administration successfully crafted the narrative of Black "welfare queens," suggesting that Black women were deliberately misusing government funds. This narrative further linked Black people to untrustworthiness. In its pursuit of health care reform—which eventually failed—the Clinton administration took the lead from the preceding president by making deep cuts to social welfare programs.

This article does not detail how these health care programs may have treated other types of minorities. According to the National Center for Farmworker Health, Inc.'s 2013-2014 survey, 73 percent of all agricultural workers were foreign born, with 69 percent of them having been born in Mexico.[248] Of all crop workers, 47 percent were unauthorized, meaning they were likely undocumented immigrants. The likelihood of them not receiving proper health care was quite high.

A searing *New York Times* op-ed, written by a Guatemalan Migrant Agricultural Worker and Organizer Alma Patty Tzalain, mentions the challenges she faces in obtaining

---

248 "Agricultural Worker Demographics," *National Center for Farmworker Health, Inc.,* 2018.

health care because of her status and race.[249] In the article she writes, "Many farmworkers don't have health insurance and aren't sure how to afford medical care or support families if we can't work. If we get sick, what will happen to us? Will we be fired because we're no longer useful to the farm and are now a threat to the business?"

Previous chapters in this book have indicated the same with respect to discrimination. For example, LGBTQ+ people have a higher likelihood of being uninsured; once they even make it to the doctors' office, they may face discrimination, especially if they are transgender and/or people of color.

In the examples above, some of the policies were directly related to health care while some were not. What does that mean for the United States?

Racism doesn't just exist in staid rooms where policies are written and passed. Porter writes that racism continues to exist at the core of America's social compact. Questions around race continue to polarize an America where Black and Brown people have felt the brunt of the violence of centuries; in this same America, many white Americans are hurting from lack of economic opportunity and seeing their towns ravaged by the opioid epidemic.

That's why, according to Porter, "racial animosity" is at the root of the United States being the only wealthy nation that doesn't provide comprehensive health care for its citizens.

---

249 Alma Patty Tzalain, "I Harvest Your Food. Why Isn't My Health 'Essential'?" *The New York Times,* April 15, 2020.

Per Porter's analysis, racism is at the center of all policy—not just health care. What does that mean for how we design policy in the future?

It is necessary for policymakers to align stakeholders around the same goal, which needs to go beyond just improving the quality of life for the average American. It is about centering and recognizing how the different isms and phobias—racism, sexism, homophobia, xenophobia, transphobia, discrimination against the poor and rural—play a role in how current health care systems operate.

For example, how has tying welfare reform to an image of a needy and greedy Black community affected Medicaid expansion and access to America's poor? How has positioning Latine Americans, particularly undocumented ones, as job stealers affected how we treat agricultural workers and those on the lowest rungs of the social ladder? How has treating Asian Americans as the "model minority" affected their ability to access health care, especially if they are low income?

Those in positions of political power should recognize policies that aren't working and commit to either reforming or subverting, in the case of Dr. Mitchell Katz. Ensuring that policymaking aligns health care's many stakeholders—pharmacy benefit managers, pharmaceutical companies, health technology (including electronic health records companies), and others—by paying close attention to important trends is critical, per the advice of Dr. Jon Burroughs.

And putting the people who matter—everyday Americans who have been forgotten and ignored by the very systems that are supposed to treat and heal them—in the center is perhaps the most important part.

CHAPTER 12

HEALTH CARE PROFILES IN COURAGE: HEALTH CARE WORKERS SUPPORTING VULNERABLE COMMUNITIES

"The more we see health as a practice rather than as a problem to fix, the more we encourage the body's natural potential to be healthy."

AARTI PATEL, AUTHOR OF *THE ART OF HEALTH: SIMPLE AND POWERFUL KEYS FOR CREATING HEALTH IN YOUR LIFE*

Before he ran for president, John F. Kennedy won a Pulitzer prize for writing *Profiles in Courage*. With extensive help from close advisor Ted Sorensen, Kennedy wrote short biographies of senators who defied party lines and suffered politically for doing what they thought was right.

Throughout my time writing this book, I had the chance to speak to so many people in health care, from medical students to board certified physicians, from health administration managers to nurses, and beyond. I am grateful to share the stories of some of those people below. Some of these people are incredibly courageous as well—many have worked on the frontlines of COVID-19. Many more are committed to thinking critically about social inclusion. We talked about COVID-19, social and health equity, and how we need to move forward.

Here are their stories.

***

As a young pharmacy student in California, Janelle Sauz thought she would be able to make a difference. Studying pharmacy in undergrad, expanding her network to include pharmacists as mentors, and gaining pharmacy technician work experience all seemed like the right things to do to get her foot in the door. But after a few years, she noticed a pattern.

"We had a lot of patients who would return for preventable conditions. I remember thinking there have to be different ways that we can combat diabetes or hypertension ... there have to be some lifestyle changes that we can encourage patients to have better health behaviors," Sauz said in an interview.

Sauz started paying attention to the information she had access to as a pharmacy technician. Perhaps, she thought, using medical information about the patient in dispensing prescriptions might help reduce the rate at which patients were coming back for preventable conditions. But upon looking at what she had access to, she realized, "You only see their medication history; you don't see their physical history; you don't see their medical history. You don't see any of the information doctors collect."

With this in the back of her mind, Janelle began preparing to apply to pharmacy doctorate programs. One application specifically asked, "What did you do to address health disparities?" Dumbfounded, Sauz said, "I remember thinking I've done nothing. I don't think I've done anything to really understand the communities I'm serving."

That was the pivotal moment when Sauz decided that pharmacy school was not the right path for her. She wanted to make a difference by being on the front lines of the fight against health care disparities among marginalized communities. This inspired her to apply to AmeriCorps, a voluntary civil service program funded by the US federal government in conjunction with foundations and donors. AmeriCorps was explicitly designed to engage adults with vulnerable parts of American society, with a commitment to "helping others and meeting critical needs in the community."

After having worked at a pharmacy in predominantly white, affluent Huntington Beach, Janelle received her Ameri-Corps assignment: managing wellness programs at a Federally Qualified Health Center (FQHC) in East Oakland. The first thing Janelle noticed was the difference between her patients in Huntington Beach and in East Oakland. These differences, she realized, stemmed from the neighborhoods that her patients lived in. During her AmeriCorps stint—which later turned into a full-time role managing population health—Janelle noticed the difference between East Oakland and San Leandro, the neighboring town where she lived.

"If you were standing at the intersection of San Leandro and East Oakland, if you're facing San Leandro, there's trees lining up the street, there's concrete that's paved, and there's lots of mom and pop shops everywhere," Sauz commented. The story was not the same with East Oakland, commonly known as a neighborhood where it wasn't safe to walk alone. "The health disparities are right here in front of us."

At the FQHC, Sauz enjoyed getting to know her patients, encouraging wellness, and running different programs that would serve their needs. Ensuring that patients experiencing homelessness had access to hot showers, that patients facing food insecurity had healthy food, and that those experiencing chronic conditions had access to classes that would help them manage their pain were just some parts of her work. She also tried to analyze health care outcomes data across the fourteen primary care clinics that her FQHC was operating to determine best practices and areas of growth.

But another problem persisted.

Despite recognizing the need to prioritize people's health and well-being, it was challenging for the FQHC, as well as most hospitals and health systems, to think about transitioning from being reimbursed based on volume (number of patients) to being reimbursed based on value (health care outcomes). According to Sauz, "During my time there, there was a lot of talk about—we're shifting from fee-for-service to value-based care, but no one really knew or understood how that was going to happen." Understanding what that transition should look like, ensuring positive operating margins, and underscoring the provision of high-quality health care are all pieces in the health care puzzle that have not been thought through as deeply.

The transition from volume to value-based care has been a conversation lasting decades. After the passage of the Affordable Care Act, it has been easier for the American health care system to realize value-based care for certain populations, such as those on public payers with chronic conditions or those insured by managed care. However, it is largely still just that: a conversation.

Sauz identified a still-broader challenge, however, with our current provision of health care. While there is no doubt that those working in community health clinics care very deeply about the challenges that the most vulnerable among their patients face, Sauz indicated not all staff in public health and medicine have the right vocabulary to define their patients' challenges within a more systemic context.

And she wouldn't be wrong.

***

While Sauz's tales of caring for patients facing adversity are strictly anecdotal, there is much evidence to back up how race and socioeconomic status intersect to prevent proper access to health care. Unfortunately, in neighborhoods like East Oakland, it is not uncommon for children to face great challenges in their lives: losing loved ones to violence on the streets in economically depressed, unsafe areas and experiencing feelings of neglect and abandonment when caregivers are working multiple jobs to support the family, among others. Adversities such as domestic violence, abuse, neglect, trauma, parental issues, and divorce are all considered adverse childhood experiences (ACEs).[250] These adverse childhood experiences are then measured through an ACE survey delivered to adults. For each adversity the respondent says they've experienced, their ACE score goes up by one.

And the results were shocking.

According to Dr. Nadine Burke Harris's acclaimed TED talk, the higher your ACE score, the worse your health outcomes.[251] If you're an individual with an ACE score of four or more, your relative risk of chronic obstructive pulmonary disease is two and a half times that of someone with an ACE score of zero. If you have an ACE score of seven or more, you have three and half times the risk of ischemic heart disease, which is the number one killer in the United States.

---

250 Burke-Harris, Nadine. "How childhood trauma affects health across a lifetime." Filmed November 2014 in San Francisco, CA. TEDMED video, 15:51.
251 Ibid.

Why does this occur? Because, when experiencing chronic adversity, the body's stress response system starts to become taxed. Over time, this can contribute to increased stress, which can cause higher risk in getting chronic conditions like heart disease.

Perhaps most importantly, the higher someone's ACE score, the more likely he or she is to engage in high-risk behaviors such as smoking, drinking, and taking addictive drugs. However, what was previously chalked up to strictly "bad behavior" now has a basis in science. Adversity can affect developing brains, meaning that when a child experiences adversity, areas of the brain related to pleasure and reward are negatively affected. Adversity inhibits the growth of the prefrontal cortex, which is essential for impulse control and learning.

Typically, providers are taught to view experiences like adverse childhood events as strictly social or mental health problems that require referral accordingly. But exposure to the ACEs study helped Burke Harris identify the best way to use this science for prevention and treatment. Working at the Center for Youth Wellness in San Francisco, she was able to encourage the use of ACEs during regular pediatric visits. If a child has a particularly high score, the center deploys a multidisciplinary team that supports the child and their family with home visits, care coordination, mental health support, and other interventions that can help reduce the child's exposure to adversity. The center ensures parents receive the right education about ACEs to encourage the development of safe home environments.

While integrating some aspects of mental health during primary care visits is not a novel idea, it is one that has had a demonstrable impact and should be adopted more widely across the nation.

While children in impoverished American communities face challenges during their growing years, so do their mothers when they are bringing life into the world. In particular, Black mothers suffer greatly when it comes to experiencing negative health care outcomes. Several decades after childbirth has moved from the home to the hospital, the United States is the only developed country with the unique distinction of rising maternal mortality rates.[252]

Black women are three to four times more likely to die in childbirth, regardless of socioeconomic status. Justified in a variety of ways, this disparity has persisted throughout American history. In the 1980s, Black women's maternal mortality was blamed on lifestyle choices of getting addicted to crack cocaine, having too many children, and living in risky neighborhoods. Stereotypes about the welfare queen and angry Black women have abounded since that time period, resulting not only in less empathy for Black patients but an implicit bias against them.[253, 254]

252 Suzanne Delbanco, Maclaine Lehan, Thi Montalvo, and Jeffrey Levin-Scherz, "The Rising U.S. Maternal Mortality Rate Demands Action from Employers," *Harvard Business Review,* June 28, 2019.

253 Christopher Borrelli, "Reagan used her, the country hated her. Decades later, the Welfare Queen of Chicago refuses to go away," *Chicago Tribune,* June 10, 2019.

254 "Jim Crow Museum of Racist Memorabilia: The Sapphire Caricature," *Ferris State University,* 2012.

Black women in pain are less likely to be taken seriously, which many times ends in fatal results. One such woman is famed tennis star Serena Williams.[255] Arguably one of the most decorated female tennis players of all time, Williams experienced breathing issues after giving birth to her daughter in 2017. Knowing that she had a history of blood clots, she asked a floor nurse for a CT scan and a heparin drip. After being dismissed, she got the attention of a physician who decided to order an ultrasound and ignore her concerns about the difficulty she was having breathing. After many minutes of persistence and self-advocacy, Williams underwent a CT scan, which found that her lungs were filled with blood clots. Then convinced, the physician connected Williams to a heparin drip.

Williams was able to advocate for herself given her education, income, and status. But what about Black mothers who aren't able to do so? Colorado-based labor and delivery nurse Katrina Little shared the story of her mother, a warm-hearted Black woman from Texas coming in after having given birth to her first child.[256] At twenty-two, she complained of excessive bleeding and was immediately recommended sterilization by way of hysterectomy. Little's mother was considered a walking stereotype: low-income Black woman from a large family with low educational attainment. According to the doctors that saw her in that Texas hospital, she didn't need to be consulted on this life-changing surgery.

255 Maya Salam, "For Serena Williams, Childbirth Was a Harrowing Ordeal. She's Not Alone." *The New York Times,* January 11, 2018.

256 Little, Katrina. "The Dying Mothers, Sisters, Daughters, Friends," Filmed September 2019 in Denver, CO. TEDxMSUDenver video, 13:50.

According to Little, "A generation of unconscious bias and purposeful or unintentional ignoring the voice of the underserved and underrepresented can affect those to come."

***

Some, like New York-based emergency room physician Dr. Olumide Akindutire, serving underserved communities through medicine was personal.

While Dr. Akindutire, who identifies as Nigerian American, now recognizes the importance of diversity in recruiting and retaining medical students, he remembers not caring in college. But by the time he got to SUNY Downstate Medical Center—located in Brooklyn—for medical school, he was treating a wide swathe of patients. He described how a majority of his patients "just didn't have the knowledge or insight to not only apply for insurance, to make follow up calls with physicians, to fill their prescriptions. So, in that, I saw complications that could have easily been preventable."

In the emergency room, it almost feels as if everyone is equal. Dr. Akindutire was quick to qualify that the statement, "'The emergency room is a sort of equalizer' isn't entirely accurate; but it does highlight that emergency room physicians are working with all different types of patients." In his words, "If you walk into an ER, you're going to get treated." In the ER, Dr. Akindutire learned the differences between the haves and the have-nots.

Most critically, Dr. Akindutire saw these differences accentuated by COVID-19. "COVID-19 has highlighted these complications because it's more serious in marginalized communities. In Detroit, for example, the Black community is much more heavily impacted. It's not only because of access to health care but also access to testing. It's also because of the kinds of policies we've made in the past eighty years."

Dr. Akindutire also spoke about the frustrations of health disparities among communities of color resurfacing and surprising people. He recalled the story of a young Black woman who was routinely denied COVID-19 testing only to be diagnosed with it and finally lose her life as a result.[257] Upon hearing about this story, his immediate reaction was, "This is not new. This is a story I've seen all the time. I've seen fellow doctors, and I know I've done this too, because we all have biases, make assumptions. I've seen people make assumptions about Black patients because of what they're wearing or how they're speaking, which unfortunately determines the level of treatment they receive."

It is challenging to overcome internal bias, but Dr. Akindutire said he seeks to treat every patient like he would treat his mother. He also recognized that a lot of patients, specifically lower-income ones, may become upset and yell at physicians because they have no voice in other parts of their life. At the end of the day, as he says, "It's my job to just help them out."

---

257 Arielle Mitropoulos and Mariya Moseley, "Beloved Brooklyn Teacher, 30, diees of coronavirus after she was twice denied a COVID-19 test," *ABC News,* April 28, 2020.

With respect to bias, Dr. Akindutire talked about the focus on social determinants of health in medical school programs. While his school, SUNY Downstate, was committed to recruiting diverse students and focusing on social determinants, he did share that may not be the case in other schools. Things have definitely changed since he was in medical school, with an increasing emphasis on social status and how it impacts access to care. However, for Dr. Akindutire, personal, lived experiences push him to want to deliver better care for patients. Being viewed with suspicion at the emergency room when he has gone as a patient is one small example of why Dr. Akindutire wants to ensure equal treatment—and respect—for every patient that walks through the doors.

The level of surprise has seemed to reach policymakers and health officials at the highest echelons of government too. Per Dr. Akindutire, government officials and those who did not understand the challenges of systemic discrimination are now waking up: "Now we have to pay attention to these basic health disparity issues when those have been the reality for people who look like us for a very long time."

***

Dr. Ramon Jacobs-Shaw has existed at the nexus of three different identity groups, which he uses to inform his experience as a practicing physician. Dr. Jacobs-Shaw identifies as Native American, gay, and growing up low-income and rural. Talking about his lived experiences growing up, he shared he is a member of the Lumbee tribe in North Carolina, which is not federally recognized. As a result, he and his family did not have health insurance (only federally recognized tribes have their health care covered through the Indian Health Service).

In an interview, Dr. Jacobs-Shaw shared, "So healthcare was definitely a privilege growing up, right? Back then it wasn't a choice to go to doctors; it would have only been out of pure necessity."

When Dr. Jacobs-Shaw graduated medical school in 2002, social determinants were not explicitly discussed in medical school classrooms. "If you had a passion for things like homelessness or impacting certain populations, that was on an individual level—you maybe worked in the free clinic. It was not discouraged, but it was not encouraged." Moreover, Dr. Jacobs-Shaw noted, his medical school class was not very diverse. He was the only Native American in his graduating class of 140 students, and Black students made up about 15 percent of the student body.

This brings up an important point for Dr. Jacobs-Shaw, that people who are from disenfranchised populations tend to want to seek care from people who look like them. This anecdotal evidence is further corroborated by a study profiled by NPR's Hidden Brain podcast. According to researcher Owen Garrick and his colleagues, Black men were more likely to take preventative services—invasive tests for diabetes, the flu, and cardiovascular diseases—more seriously when treated by a Black doctor.[258]

---

258 Shankar Vedantam, Jennifer Schmidt, Parth Shah, Tara Boyle, and Rhaina Cohen "People Like Us: How Our Identities Shape Health And

Dr. Jacobs-Shaw identified the root of better responding to a doctor of the same racial or ethnic background is due to mistreatment in the system, which has been echoed in previous chapters. According to him, "If you are a Native American, you have lots of distrust for westernized medicine. If you are from an African American background, there's lots of distrust, dating back to just a couple of decades ago, for example, with the Tuskegee Airmen. If you're from an LGBTQ+ background, you've been told by medicine that you're dysfunctional and have mental illness, as recently as a few years ago. So why would you trust the system?" Dr. Jacobs-Shaw has also commented on the woeful pipelines for physicians from diverse backgrounds that need to be strengthened at a national level.

But as someone who had seen firsthand the consequences of challenges to health care access, Dr. Jacobs-Shaw not only wants to practice medicine, but to keep health care disparities front and center. In 2011, this interest was brought more directly into the workplace when Dr. Jacobs-Shaw joined efforts to create an LGBTQ+ Council for employees.

Beyond lived experiences, Dr. Jacobs-Shaw wants to improve care for the patients he serves: "I was interested in the [disparities] work from what I was seeing in my own patients: hearing their stories about bias and discrimination, for LGBTQ+ but also for other patients, like immigrants, African Americans, fellow Native Americans, and women in terms of the sexism they encounter."

Educational Success," June 3, 2019 in *Hidden Brain*, produced by NPR, MP3 audio, 35:24.

It is also important to note how keenly zip codes in the United States are tied to destiny. As Dr. Jacobs-Shaw astutely pointed out, "The zip code that you live in could really outline a lot of things. If you're able to afford living in a zip code that affords you world class healthcare, it's probably based on a whole lot of other social determinants, like education. Did you complete college? If you did, you have access to certain types of employment that pay better."

All of these domino effects, broadly categorized as social determinants of health, so clearly impact health outcomes. Where people live is clearly tied to the not-so-long-ago legacy of segregation. And as legal scholar and author of *The Color of Law* Richard Rothstein so clearly points out, "Today's residential segregation in the North, South, Midwest, and West is not the unintended consequence of individual choices and of otherwise well-meaning law or regulation but of unhidden public policy that explicitly segregated every metropolitan area in the United States."[259]

Aside from public policy, technology is often touted as another barrier between those who can access great care and those who cannot. When talking about health care technology, the American public is used to hearing about the latest cutting-edge products available in the health space as a result of Silicon Valley. However, we are less likely to hear about how those products will reach neighborhoods like South Central Los Angeles, Harlem in New York City, and the South Side of Chicago in a meaningful way.

---

259 "The Color of Law: A Forgotten History of How Our Government Segregated America," *Economic Policy Institute,* 2017.

According to Dr. Jacobs-Shaw, "What's so slow to happen within health care is that health care has to actually prove that it exists before something is actually done." It is critical to prove, anecdotally and empirically, that bias and discrimination play a role in how marginalized communities receive care. With this in mind, Dr. Jacobs-Shaw had this to say about balancing the contradictions of how quickly technology moves and how slowly research is developed.

> *"The dynamic within healthcare is… is one of contradiction. One, the pace of change of things like biotech, new medications, new technologies, move at a superfast pace. The practicality of some of those things actually hitting hospitals or clinics or patient care is slower. Also, research is slow moving, right? So, if you notice something that is wrong, like racism, or bias or discrimination that exists within healthcare, we've known that now for a long time. But to actually get the buy-in of leadership within the healthcare arena is another thing. Right?"*

In his current role as senior medical director at new primary care enterprise Oak Street Health, Dr. Jacobs-Shaw described the "patchwork of health services" that are offered to people of color and lower-income folks—and to all Americans.[260] Along with bias and discrimination, lower-income people have to deal with under-resourced or unevenly funded insurance coverage plans. For example, those who have their healthcare covered under the Indian Health Service have

---

260 Rhea Patel, "Walmart and Oak Street Health launch joint health clinics," *Business Insider*, September 4, 2020.

very poor outcomes. This knowledge has in part driven Dr. Jacobs-Shaw to join Oak Street Health, to make primary care more accessible to people of all ages, but especially those above the age of sixty-five.

Dr. Jacobs-Shaw stressed about the IHS that "it's funded worse than Medicaid. It's not even funded to the level that was promised when the IHS was initially launched." Americans using Medicaid to obtain care have highly disparate experiences depending on how much funding Medicaid is given in that state in a particular year. Constant lawsuits against the ACA can sometimes be confusing to follow, making it unclear what health care insurance is permissible and what isn't.[261] This lack of consistency across our health policy—which seems largely dictated by politics—creates lasting challenges in addressing systemic access issues for marginalized communities.

This lack of continuity of health care occurs because of competing interests among stakeholders, which creates unmanageable amounts of complexity. This complexity has had long-term consequences for the most vulnerable in the United States.

Which is why Dr. Jacobs-Shaw is determined to understand— and expand—this patchwork of health care so it works for all Americans.

---

261 MaryBeth Musumeci, "Explaining California v. Texas: A Guide to the Case Challenging the ACA," *Kaiser Family Foundation,* September 1, 2020.

***

Graduating from medical school in 2020 was supposed to be like any other year. But for recent New York College of Medicine graduate Aparna Panja, it most definitely was not. While she and her classmates had to endure weeks of Zoom classes after being pulled out their clinical rotations, they sought to graduate early to join the fight against COVID-19. For a few weeks, Panja volunteered at a COVID-19 testing site near Westchester Medical Center by calling patients to share their COVID-19 diagnoses with them. While sharing positive diagnoses with patients and encouraging them to self-isolate for fourteen days, a very common response was: "How am I going to isolate with everything I have going on?"

For patients who are the primary caretakers of children or aging parents or relatives who don't speak English, self-isolating, especially in apartments, did not feel like an option. Panja pointed out, "If one person is tested positive in the household, and that person is the caretaker, the one who normally goes out to get groceries or goes out to work, they're the ones holding everything together. When that person is taken out and told to self-isolate, the whole system crashes."

To add to this, Panja pointed out the challenge of asking members of marginalized communities to isolate in tight quarters. She herself was sharing an apartment in the Bronx with four classmates and wondered how families in one-bedroom apartments could be expected to do the same.

Panja discussed the importance of spending power among COVID-19 patients. While she had friends who started ordering groceries using HelloFresh or Amazon Fresh, she recognized that large families, especially those who are low income, may be unable to bulk order groceries because of expenses and lack of storage space.

In medical school, Panja has learned a lot about building patient trust. More importantly, according to Panja, she and her classmates have learned: "Who gets health care and why? What are the barriers? And when people get to the doctor's office, how do we build trust and be the type of doctor that can have a conversation with someone and not sound condescending?" In order to build that trust, a lot needs to be done from the physicians' end. In a searing quote, Panja said:

> *"Even though we as physicians are bringing our knowledge, care, and concern, they're [patients] bringing all of their past experiences with the health care system. Other doctors might not have listened to them, might have dismissed them. They might be telling their story for the fourth time and they're feeling like nobody's listening because they've been sent home without any answers."*

This idea of patients not being heard or feeling advocated for is not new, especially in marginalized communities. Mistrust in the medical system is rooted in previous historical experiences for many communities, particularly communities of color. Evidence continues to suggest that women who struggle with chronic pain are not believed by medical professionals.[262] However, these histories are not often taught as part of the core curriculum in medical schools. Panja pointed out that "A lot of our classes were about building trust with patients but not necessarily examining where that mistrust may come from. There are ways to learn more, but you have to seek them out."

The "old guard" of physicians might not have been taught the importance of not only social determinants of health but also other care team members—such as social workers and community health workers. Panja has shared that even though building patient trust with their circumstances in mind has been integrated into her curriculum, focusing on collaboration with social work is hard to do in early medical school education. "You know that social work is what can help a patient go home safely or transition to a skilled nursing facility. Social work is often thought of as a category of stuff someone else—a social worker—deals with later." Especially when studying for grueling exams and such, these concerns often get pushed to the back burner.

However, having a better understanding of how social workers and community health workers do their job is critical to be a good physician. While physicians are already responsible for a lot of knowledge, Panja advocates for physicians to be aware of what their team members are responsible for and how those team members can support better health outcomes.

---

262 Ashley Fetters, "The Doctor Doesn't Listen to Her. But the Media is Starting To." *The Atlantic*, August 10, 2018.

Physicians have—and continue to have—a lot on their plates. The COVID-19 pandemic and continuing challenges with racism and police violence as public health issues have not made it any easier. But physicians—along with other health care team members—are striving to provide the best that they can for their patients.

CHAPTER 13

AN ODE: TO COVID-19 AND #BLACKLIVESMATTER

———

"What the world needs now is solidarity. With solidarity we can defeat the virus and build a better world."
—UNITED NATIONS SECRETARY-GENERAL ANTÓNIO GUTERRES

"All our silences in the face of racist assault are acts of complicity."
—BELL HOOKS

Throughout the book, two key moments and movements have been referenced time and time again. One is the COVID-19 pandemic that has ravaged much of the world since December 2019 and continues to do so many months later. What started as a completely misunderstood illness in Wuhan, China, quickly enveloped the world in a matter of months. Americans watched in horror as the disease spread throughout Asia, hit the Princess Cruise Line cruise ship (aboard which were some US citizens), and finally hit American shores.

The first case in the United States was detected in a nursing home based in Kirkland, Washington, but before long, the disease had spread to other parts of the United States.[263] Some states acted quickly—Governor Gavin Newsom of California issued a stay-at-home order directed at more than 40 million California residents as early as March 19th.[264] Some moved more gradually—Governor Ron DeSantis did not issue an executive order directing Floridians to stay home until April 1st, after further consultation from the White House.

Despite some precautions, New York City was ravaged by the pandemic in March and April, resulting in the deaths of thousands of people at a time when clinicians did not always know how to save lives.[265] In particular, those living in diverse, low-income communities—Jackson Heights in Queens boasts the most linguistic diversity in the country, with 167 languages being spoken there—were hit hardest by the pandemic's economic and health consequences.[266]

---

263 Jack Healy and Serge Kovaleski, "The Coronavirus's Rampage Through a Suburban Nursing Home," *The New York Times,* May 21, 2020.

264 Office of Governor Gavin Newsom, "Governor Gavin Newsom Issues Stay at Home Order," *CA.gov,* March 19, 2020.

265 Eric Levenson, "Why New York is the epicenter of the American coronavirus outbreak," *CNN,* March 26, 2020.

266 The New York Times, "Block by Block: Jackson Heights," *The New York Times,* November 17, 2015.

Not much is known about the disease, with mixed messaging coming from public health officials in the United States and around the world.

As late as early June 2020, the World Health Organization made a statement that it thought that asymptomatic transmission of the disease was very rare, only to walk back those statements a few days later.[267] In the United States, important federal agencies like the Centers for Disease Control waffled on important protocols as late as August 2020, deeming that those who were asymptomatic would not require testing.[268] While Dr. Anthony Fauci and Dr. Deborah Birx provided valuable information at what were once daily presidential press briefings; those same press briefings increasingly politicized the virus and shared some false information.[269]

This continued to erode trust in American public health messaging and institutions, and yet increased respect for frontline clinical staff who were doing their best to save lives with limited personal protective equipment (PPE) and ventilators.[270, 271] Though New Yorkers clapped and banged pots and pans to celebrate the work of clinicians—doctors, nurses, respiratory therapists, social workers, and others—and to

267 Andrew Joseph, "'We don't actually have that answer yet': WHO clarifies comments on asymptomatic spread of Covid-19," *Stat,* June 9, 2020.

268 Katherine Wu, "C.D.C. Now Says People Without Covid-19 Symptoms Do Not Need Testing," *The New York Times,* September 17, 2020.

269 Karen Travers and Jordyn Phelps, "Trump using daily crisis briefings to stay in the political spotlight," *ABC News,* April 9, 2020.

270 Adam Jeffery, "New Yorkers stop and give daily thanks and gratitude for coronavirus frontline workers," *CNBC,* April 10, 2020.

271 Chris Dall, "As pandemic rages, PPE supply remains a problem," *Center for Infectious Disease and Research Policy News,* July 29, 2020.

recognize their valiant efforts, *The New York Post* published an article sharing that staff at a hospital near Columbus Circle—an affluent neighborhood in Manhattan—resorted to wearing trash bags because they were out of hospital gowns.

Those images continue to be emblazoned in the minds of states that struggled with overwhelmed hospitals and morgues in the earlier part of 2020. States that suffered from increased COVID-19 pandemic cases earlier in the year had robust messaging campaigns around masks, social distancing, and opening and closing certain businesses. However, there are still other states where those impacts currently remain. Many of those states grace the list of travel advisories in states that suffered earlier on. In New Jersey alone, thirty-five states have been added—and re-added—to the travel advisory list.[272]

Living in 2020 has made working from home, wearing masks, socially distancing, and avoiding large indoor gatherings the norm. Now, cities and towns are planning for another devastating economic hit as outdoor seating becomes unavailable in the colder fall and winter months in the north.

Then, in May, a second pandemic—that had always been simmering under the surface—hit America in a raw, unfettered way. The murder of George Floyd at the hands of the Minneapolis police department exploded across television and social media, causing immense outrage and frustration. While the murders of Ahmaud Arbery and Breonna

---

272 Official Site of the State of New Jersey, "New Jersey COVID-19 Information Hub," *NJ.gov*, 2020.

Taylor—with the latter's grand jury trial resulting in incredibly disappointing news—had brought similar feelings earlier in the summer, the image of George Floyd with a police officer's knee on his neck in broad daylight highlighted the tensions between the Black community and law enforcement. Many mask-wearing protestors came out onto the street to push back against racial injustice in nearly every city and town in America; some were unfortunately met with police violence. Looting of businesses on the street brought back memories of the well-publicized 1992 Watts riots in Los Angeles after the beating of Rodney King—resulting in similar arguments between business owners, protestors, and others.

These twin pandemics—one emerging in recent months and one stretching out as long as time—continue to devastate marginalized communities, especially those of color.

***

Very early on in the COVID-19 pandemic, rumors started to spread that Black people were immune from this new strain of coronavirus. False information about the zero cases of COVID-19 in Africa began to spread, making it seem that Black people had nothing to worry about as this virus spread across the world and the United States.[273] However, city health departments and celebrities like British actor Idris

---

273 The Editors, "Too Many Black Americans Are Dying from COVID-19," *Scientific American,* August 1, 2020.

Elba jumped to action, publishing articles and videos that ran counter to these dangerous rumors.

Moreover, the reality in the United States started to bear out differently. Black, Indigenous, and Latine individuals were disproportionately affected by the pandemic, and the reasons behind this disparity are incredibly layered. Because of discriminatory policies in the past—explained in the book thus far—access to economic opportunity that would otherwise allow these communities to work from home, collect severance, or live in well-ventilated, spacious housing was not very common.

People of color and lower-income individuals are less likely to have supportive work environments with generous leave policies that allow them to be home when they become sick. The most infamous example of this was the Smithfield pork factory in Sioux Falls, South Dakota.[274] Once a beacon of hope for America's newly arrived refugees, who made minimum wage in a state with low costs of living but were able to send children to college and buy homes, now a factory hot spot for COVID-19.

Despite the fact that factory leaders were sounding alarm bells about crowded working conditions and lack of protective equipment, management did not respond in an adequate fashion, resulting in many deaths. South Dakota Governor Kristi Noem announced the state would not be issuing stay-at-home orders—despite the request of Sioux Falls Mayor

---

274 Caitlin Dickerson and Miriam Jordan, "South Dakota Meat Plant Is Now Country's Biggest Coronavirus Hot Spot," *The New York Times*, May 4, 2020.

Paul TenHaken—indicating it would not have made a difference since the plant would have remained open as a "critical infrastructure business."[275]

This points to another challenge that people of color and low-income people have faced during the pandemic: they are more likely to be working "essential" jobs that don't permit working from home.

The media focused on physicians, nurses, and other clinical workers as essential—which they absolutely are. Many suffered from post-traumatic stress disorder and burnout as a result of being overwhelmed with affected patients and not being equipped to take care of all of them. *The New York Times* profiled Dr. Lorna Breen, who supervised the emergency department of New York-Presbyterian Allen Hospital.[276] Faced with Black and Brown patients who were getting infected and dying in record numbers—and who did not have the resources to get tested, get masks, and stay socially distanced—Dr. Breen took her own life on April 26, 2020. It was perhaps the first time that those of us in the public who were not in hospitals during the pandemic could palpably feel the fear and uncertainty common in those spaces.

However, there were other essential workers—lesser paid, invisible, and not thanked often enough.

---

275 Caitlin Dickerson and Miriam Jordan, "South Dakota Meat Plant Is Now Country's Biggest Coronavirus Hot Spot," *The New York Times*, May 4, 2020.

276 Corina Knoll, Ali Watkins, and Michaeel Rothfeld, "'I Couldn't Do Anything': The Virus and an E.R. Doctor's Suicide," *The New York Times*, July 11, 2020.

Grocery store clerks, housekeepers, food service workers, home health aides, and others continued to go to work every day during the pandemic. Many had to deal with unruly, unmasked customers as well as intergenerational households, where family members were worried about infecting grandparents and immunocompromised relatives.[277, 278] Alma Patty Tzalan, a farmworker and labor organizer, wrote a searing piece in *The New York Times* titled "I Harvest Your Food. Why Isn't My Health 'Essential?'"[279] Beyond the title, Tzalan talks about being sick, testing negative for COVID-19, and not being allowed to get paid leave. She discusses using her income, much like the refugees of the Smithfield factory, to support family in the United States and her home country of Nicaragua.

How do we have limited to no protections for those who ensure we have food on the table?

***

These are just some of the obstacles that people are facing on a day-to-day basis. Yes, most vulnerable communities are essential workers who do not get the same protections as those in more white-collar professions.

---

277 Abha Bhattaral, "Retail workers are being pulled into the latest culture war: Getting customers to wear masks," *The Washington Post,* July 8, 2020.

278 "Double Jeopardy: COVID-19 and Behavioral Health Disparities for Black and Latino Communities in the U.S.," *Substance Abuse and Mental Health Services Administration,* 2020.

279 Alma Patty Tzalain, "I Harvest Your Food. Why Isn't My Health 'Essential'?" *The New York Times,* April 15, 2020.

However, as this book has detailed, so many of these challenges already existed prior to the pandemic. Vulnerable communities—particularly people of color—were more likely to live in crowded, poorly ventilated housing with many people. They are less likely to live in safe neighborhoods with green space and place for children to play. Of particular note, Indigenous communities are most likely to be disconnected from existing health care systems. As mentioned in the chapter about Native health, even those who are not on reservations struggle to find care that works for them.

All of these are interconnected by the legacies of policies written, passed, and enforced decades ago—and even more recently. These policies—intermingled with cultural narratives about certain communities—made it acceptable for health care not to be accessible to certain populations.

Forced relocation of Native Americans uprooted them from their ancestral lands and compromised their traditional, healthy ways of gathering and cooking food. Always being on the move and increasing reliance on the government for food subsidies resulted in increased rates of obesity and hypertension. Cultural narratives saying that Natives were savage and in need of civilization abounded, justifying family separation and forced assimilation among Native children.

This contributed to intergenerational trauma and mental health issues seen in Native communities. Today, the history of Native Americans being uprooted throughout the United States gets one or two paragraphs in American history textbooks, leaving many to believe they largely no longer exist. Now, however, more Native Americans are preserving their heritage, celebrating their traditions, and reclaiming their narratives.

Source: Pupils at Carlisle Indian Industrial School, Pennsylvania—a boarding school where Native American children were forced to assimilate and separated from their parents—in 1900.[280]

Slavery and segregation shaped the ways in which Black Americans arrived and lived in this country for centuries, with additional policies, laws, and court cases determining their lack of equality compared to white Americans. Dangerous stereotypes accompanied these policies, introducing American society to "brutish, savagely strong Blacks," "Black welfare queens," "angry Black women," and "sexually aggressive Black men who were a threat around white women."

---

280 "Pupils at Carlisle Indian Industrial School, Pennsylvania (c.1900)," Public Domain, September 16, 2008.

These stereotypes contributed not only to negative images of the Black community but have also fundamentally shaped how Black bodies are viewed in medicine. It became common for many to think Black people are immune to pain and illness. Moreover, immigrants coming from Africa and the Caribbean start to suffer worse health outcomes after being exposed to racial discrimination and stress post-emigration.

Now the #BlackLivesMatter movement has brought the inequality of police brutality to the fore, starting with the publicized death of Michael Brown in Ferguson, Missouri, in 2014. Time and time again, when a Black person is killed unfairly at the hands of the police, people united on the streets and on social media under this hashtag to demand accountability and change. This has been even more true in May of 2020, after police officers in Minneapolis, kneeled on the neck of George Floyd, ultimately killing him. While the pandemic raged on, big cities and small towns alike hosted rallies, protests, and marches in solidarity with Black lives.

How does this connect to health care? The flicker of fear, an increased heart rate, and sweaty palms might be some signs that a Black person exhibits when hearing the sound of a police car or anticipating watching a video of a Black person facing violence. The biological repercussions of racism and discrimination regularly rear their ugly heads—when someone faces an act of overt or covert racism, their body might respond with increased cortisol levels and increased heart rate.[281] When the body is exposed to this type of chronic stress, it might be more likely to get heart disease. According to Mental Health America, vicarious traumatic stressors can add race-related stress to other communities as well.[282] For example, Native American children are vicariously traumatized by seeing high rates of suicide, homicide, and drug addiction in their communities.

And those are just two examples.

Source: Flickr[283]

***

281 Rae Ellen Bichell, "Scientists Start to Tease Out The Subtler Ways Racism Hurts Health," *NPR,* November 11, 2017.

282 "Racial Trauma," *Mental Health America* website, June 25, 2020.

283 Dan Aasland, "Protesters in Minneapolis, Minnesota where George Floyed was killed and the unrest began," Wikipedia images, May 29, 2020.

Outside of Black and Indigenous communities, other racial, ethnic, and social groups have faced systemic damage at the hands of American policy and cultural narratives.

Asian Americans—particularly East Asians—have experienced even higher levels of racism because of the COVID-19 pandemic. The pandemic originated in Wuhan, China, resulting in many East Asians across the world facing bullying and harassment from others. As health policy researcher Matthew Lee explains in an *NBC* article, East Asians have conveniently flipped between being the "yellow peril"—dangerous, scheming, and conniving—and the "model minority"—the healthiest, wealthiest, most hardworking non-white people America has to offer.[284] The change of narrative typically happens whenever it is most convenient for the current political moment.

South Asians have had to undergo the challenges of policing and surveillance post-9/11 while also balancing the model minority myth in their own right. Southeast Asians—Vietnamese and Filipino communities in particular—have had to reckon with US militarization in their own countries and being largely forgotten in broader narratives about Asians in American society. And those who were perhaps the most forgotten—Native Hawaiians, the Chamorro people of Guam, and others—are largely left out of conversations about identity and belonging in American society.

---

284 Matthew Lee, "Coronavirus fears show how 'model minority' Asian Americans become the 'yellow peril,'" *NBC,* March 9, 2020.

Source: PBS[285]

The model minority myth conflates all of these narratives, leaving out serious health disparities different Asian communities experience. Perhaps more importantly, the model minority myth prevents these communities from accessing the health care resources they need.

Colonization has largely characterized those who identify as Latine American. After centuries of European conquest and an increase in US involvement with the war on drugs, many from Latin America journeyed to the United States in search of a better life. However, given discriminatory policy against immigrants from these countries—particularly those who are undocumented—it has been challenging for this community to access necessary health care.

Rules like the public charge rule have made it challenging for people to enroll in Medicaid and get care for them and their children. The way that Medicaid runs—decisions made by state governments—truly indicates that geography dictates

---

285 "Asian Americans," *PBS Thirteen* website, 2020.

destiny. Those who live in states with less generous Medicaid programs—and less strategic COVID-19 planning—were the ones who suffered the most.

Rural communities in America have been largely left behind as the rest of the country benefited from the trends of globalization, environmentalism, and increasing use of the internet. Getting to doctors is a challenge for those in rural America, as is the search for strong economic opportunity.

However, telemedicine and strengthened partnerships with community-based organizations may provide paths forward. Working with medical schools and training newly minted physicians on the special challenges that rural communities face can increase the pipeline, while matching doctors to communities not based on geography but on need may be incredibly useful for America's small towns and farmland.

It may be difficult to think about the large swathe of low-income people who live in the richest country in the world, because they are largely invisible. However, their inability to access health care has become increasingly known throughout the COVID-19 pandemic. Medicare and Medicaid were established as government-run health care programs that would cover the care of the elderly and those with low income, partially in response to the findings of sociologist Michael Harrington in *The Other America*. While imperfect, these programs have helped many lower-income people find access to care and improve their health outcomes. During COVID-19, these communities have been the first to lose work, the first to run out of COVID-related unemployment benefits, and the first to struggle to find their way back to financial stability.

Caption: President Jimmy Carter signing the Rural Health Clinic Services Act of 1977
Source: Wikipedia[286]

Women, while making up more than half of the US population, have been routinely subjugated to laws and policies that positioned them as second class citizens. After women—largely white women—achieved the right to vote in 1920, women had to continue to fight for the right to open bank accounts on their own, do meaningful work outside the home, and rise in the ranks of male-dominated fields.

There has been a long history of not believing women when they share their struggles, health care or otherwise. This

286 White House Staff Photographers, "President Carter signing the Rural Health Clinic Services Act in the Oval Office, Washington, DC, December 13, 1977," Wikipedia images, April 12, 2012.

lack of belief is further compounded for women of color and Black women in particular. The lack of inclusion of women in clinical trials has meant lesser research on how medication impacts women's bodies, having lasting ramifications for health. During the COVID-19 pandemic, we have seen how women have had to increasingly take on household chores, childcare, and tending to the sick. Described as the "mental load," responsibilities of the home and hearth have piled up during the pandemic, making it more challenging for women to put their own health first.[287] Thanks to journalists like Maya Dusenbery, women are learning how to advocate for themselves in doctors' offices and push to be included in data collection around health outcomes.

In a largely heteronormative society, those who identify as LGBTQ+ have been stepped on and marginalized. From federal policies defining what marriage is, to the fear of being outed and losing one's job, to being openly beaten to death, this community has had to face all the odds for just existing.

Since the Stonewall Uprising, LGBTQ+ community members have continued to push forward to advocate for themselves and their rights. The AIDS crisis in the 1980s was the first time the LGBTQ+ community had to reckon with a serious health issue that affected them first. Since that time, LGBTQ+ individuals have had to grapple with bias and discrimination in doctors' offices and other health care touchpoints. Thankfully, tech companies like Plume are making it easier for trans people to access hormone therapy and advocates are

---

287 Emma, "The gender wars of household chores: a feminist comic," *The Guardian,* May 26, 2017.

continuing to push forward to ensure that LGBTQ+ people can live healthier lives.

As we've seen, our identity markers largely shape our lived experiences. You can hold multiple identities at once, as professor Kimberlé Crenshaw pointed out when she coined the term "intersectionality." The reason behind these markers are largely historical—the legacies of the past affect how we currently access, consume, and pay for our health care. These legacies cause many to experience the health care of a thousand slights; to suffer from not just bias and discrimination at the doctor's office but to suffer from other inequities that make it hard to get care in the first place.

But we press on. Innovations in technology and policy can help drive the change necessary to increase access, improve outcomes, and ensure everyone in America can lead healthy, dignified lives. What also needs to accompany these innovations is a true reckoning with America's discriminatory past.

Only when we acknowledge where we've been can we get to where we are going.

APPENDIX

———

INTRODUCTION

Alameda County Health Department. "Part One: Health Equities," 2001-2005.

Horne, Madison. "Photos Reveal Shocking Conditions of Tenement Slums in the Late 1800s." *History Channel.* January 22, 2020.

Fitzsimmons, Tim. "LGBTQ History Month: The early days of America's AIDS crisis." *NBC News.* October 15, 2018.

Martin, Nina and Montagne, Renee. "Nothing Protects Black Women from Dying in Pregnancy and Childbirth." *ProPublica.* December 7, 2017.

Public Health. "HIV and AIDS: An Origin Story." Accessed on April 4, 2020.

CHAPTER 1: THE FIRST PEOPLE

Alaska Native Tribal Health Consortium. "Overview." accessed on March 27, 2020.

Burnett, Charles, dir. *Power to Heal.* Accessed on March 23, 2020.

Campbell, Alexia Fernandez. "How America's Past Shapes Native Americans' Present." *The Atlantic.* October 12, 2016.

Dodging Bullets. "Melissa Walls Ph.D. and Michelle Johnson-Jennings Ph.D. Discuss Historical Trauma." accessed March 23, 2020.

Editorial Staff. "Risks of Alcoholism Among Native Americans." *American Addiction Centers.* January 2, 2020.

Elliott, Sarah K. "How American Indian Reservations Came to Be." *PBS.* May 25, 2015.

Flores, Michael W., Benjamin Le Cook, Brian Mullin, Gabriel Halperin-Goldstein. "Associations between neighborhood-level factors and opioid-related mortality: A multi-level analysis using death certificate data," *Addiction.* (Feb 2020): 1 - 12.

Indian Health Service. "Special Diabetes Program for Indians (SDPI)," accessed on April 2, 2020.

Johns Hopkins Bloomberg School of Public Health Center for American Indian Health. "Melissa Walls." accessed on March 24, 2020.

Miller, Jen. "Frybread." *Smithsonian Magazine.* July 2008.

Morales, Laurel. "Many Native Americans Can't Get Clean Water, Report Finds." *NPR*. November 18, 2019.

National Park Service. "History & Culture."

Nathan, Kertu Tenso, and Zev Schuman-Olivier. "Associations between neighborhood-level factors and opioid-related mortality: A multi-level analysis using death certificate data." *Addiction* (February 2020): 1 - 12.

Partners in Health. "Navajo Nation: PIH serves Native Americans struggling with some of the worst health outcomes in the United States," accessed on April 2, 2020.

Poon, Linda. ""How 'Indian Relocation' Created a Public Health Crisis." *Bloomberg CityLab*, December 2, 2019.

Stejskal, Lou (loustejskal), "Aged Cheddar Rillettes—Truffle, cauliflower, fry bread, " Flickr photo, December 2, 2017.

U.S. Department of the Interior, Bureau of Indian Affairs, Indian Health Service. *Special Diabetes Program for Indians 2014 Report to Congress: Changing the Course of Diabetes: Turning Hope into Reality*, Washington DC, 2014.

U.S. Department of the Interior: Indian Affairs. "Bureau of Indian Affairs."

U.S. Federal Emergency Management Agency. "Federal Trust Responsibility."

Walls, Melissa and Les B. Whitebeck. "The Intergenerational Effects of Relocation Policies on Indigenous Families." *Journal of Family Issues.* June 14, 2012.

Walker, Mark. "Fed Up with Deaths, Native Americans Want to Run Their Own Health Care." *New York Times,* October 15, 2019.

Warne, Donald MD and Linda Bane Frizzell, PhD, "American Indian Health Policy: Historical Trends and Contemporary Issues." *American Journal of Public Health* 104, no. S3 (2014).

Whitney, Eric. "Native Americans Feel Invisible in US Health Care System." *NPR from Montana Public Radio,* December 12, 2017.

Whittle, Joe. "Most Native Americans live in cities, not reservations. Here are their stories." *The Guardian,* September 4, 2017.

Zane, Damian. "Barbie challenges the 'white saviour complex.'" *BBC,* April 30, 2016.

CHAPTER 2: WE SHALL OVERCOME

AAUW. "Dorothy Celeste Boulding Ferebee Pioneering Civil Rights and Healthcare." accessed on April 15, 2020.

Ancient Song Doula Services, "About Us," accessed on April 15, 2020.

Bassett, Mary. "#BlackLivesMatter: A Challenge to the Medical and Public Health Communities," *New England Journal of Medicine* 372 (2015).

Bassett, Mary. "Why your doctor should care about social justice." Filmed November 2015 in New York, NY. TED video, 13:42.

Black Lives Matter, "6 Years Later and Black Activists are Still Fighting: An Open Letter from Black Lives Matter Global Network Co-Founder and Strategic Advisor Patrisse Khan-Cullors," accessed on April 14, 2020.

Burnett, Charles, dir. *Power to Heal.* Accessed on March 23, 2020.

Chakraborty, Ranjani. "The US medical system is still haunted by slavery." *Vox,* December 7, 2017.

FXB Center for Health and Human Rights at Harvard University, "Mary T. Bassett MD, MPH," accessed on April 17, 2020.

Griffith, Derek M., Jonetta Johnson, Rong Zhang, Harold Neighbors, and James S. Jackson, "Ethnicity, Nativity, and the Health of American Blacks," *Journal of Healthcare for the Poor and Underserved* 22, no.1 (2011): 142-156.

Harvard Medical School Medical Education, "Alvin F. Pouissant, MD," accessed on April 13, 2020.

Henderson, Jim. "Statue of Sims in New York's Central Park, removed in April 2018," Wikipedia images, May 24, 2008.

Hlavinka, Elizabeth. "Racial Bias in Flexner Report Permeates Medical Education Today." *Medpage Today,* June 18, 2020.

Library of Congress. "W.E.B. DuBois' Hand-Drawn Infographics of African-American Life (1900)."

Maqbool, Aleem. "Coronavirus: Why has the virus hit African Americans so hard?" *BBC.* April 11, 2020.

Martin, Nina and Montagne, Renee. "Nothing Protects Black Women from Dying in Pregnancy and Childbirth." *ProPublica.* December 7, 2017.

McGrail, Stephen. "Philadelphia Negro (The)." *The Encyclopedia of Greater Philadelphia,* accessed on April 9, 2020.

NYC Department of Health and Mental Hygiene, "NYC Department of Health and Mental Hygiene - Center for Health Equity," YouTube video, October 30, 2015.

Randall, Vernellia. "Eliminating the Slave Health Deficit: Using Reparation to Repair Black Health." *Poverty & Race* 11, no. 6 (2002): 3-8, 14.

Stanford School of Medicine Ethnogeriatrics, "Health history: Up from Slavery," accessed on April 7, 2020.

Treisman, Rachel. "Whistleblower Alleges 'Medical Neglect,' Questionable Hysterectomies of ICE Detainees." *NPR,* September 16, 2020.

U.S. Centers for Disease Control and Prevention, "U.S. Public Health Service Syphilis Study at Tuskegee," accessed on April 16, 2020.

Washington, Harriet A. "First Chapter: Medical Apartheid." *The New York Times,* February 18. 2007.

White Coats for Black Lives, "Our Mission," accessed on April 15, 2020.

Whitlock, Meico. "NYC Health Commissioner Dr. Mary Bassett Receives Nicholas A. Rango Leadership Award for More Than 30 Years of Leadership in Addressing HIV-Related Inequalities," *NASTAD*, May 25, 2016.

Wortsman, Peter. "Alumni Profile: Mary T. Bassett '79 -- A Champion of Health Equity at the Helm of the NYC Department of Health," *Columbia Medicine*. accessed on April 15, 2020.

CHAPTER 3: NOT JUST A MODEL MINORITY

Adia, Alexander C., Jennifer Nazareno, Don Operario, and Ninez A. Ponce, "Health Conditions, Outcomes, and Service Access Among Filipino, Vietnamese, Chinese, Japanese, and Korean Adults in California, 2011-2017," *American Journal of Public Health* 110, no. 4 (2020): 520-526.

Berger, Joseph. "Indian, Twice Removed," *The New York Times*, December 17, 2004.

Bhattacharya, Ananya. "Indian immigrants have it bad in Donald Trump's America. But the early 1900s were worse." *Quartz*, July 16, 2019.

Celis, Tamar., "From farmer to forager: WWII CHamorus survive on family ranch, starve in concentration camp," *Pacific Daily News*, January 13, 2019.

Chin, Marshall H., "Addressing Social Needs and Structural Inequities to Reduce Health Disparities: A Call to Action for Asian American Heritage Month," *National Minority Health Month Blog* (blog), *Office of Minority Health*, May 15, 2019.

Chishti, Muzaffar, Faye Hipsman, and Isabel Ball, "Fifty Years On, the 1965 Immigration Nationality Act Continues to Reshape the United States," Migration Policy Institute, October 15, 2015.

Chow, Kat. "As Chinese Exclusion Act Turns 135, Experts Point to Parallels Today." *NPR,* May 5, 2017.

Chow, Kat. "'Model Minority' Myth Again Used As A Racial Wedge Between Asians and Blacks." *NPR,* April 19, 2017.

Constante, Agnes, "New study reveals previously invisible health issues among Asians in U.S.," *NBC News,* February 24, 2020. Accessed on April 3, 2020.

Gordon, Nancy P., Teresa Y. Lin, Jyoti Rau, and Joan C. Lo. "Aggregation of Asian-American subgroups mask meaningful differences in health and health risks among Asian ethnicities: an electronic health record based cohort study," *BMC Public Health* 19, (2019): 1 - 14.

Guo, Jeff., "The real reasons the U.S. became less racist toward Asian Americans." *The Washington Post,* November 26, 2019.

Imawasa, Gayle Y., "Recommendations for the Treatment of Asian-American/Pacific Islander Populations." *Psychological Treatment of Ethnic Minority Populations: Asian American Psychological Association.* Accessed on April 2, 2020.

Jaikaran, Elizabeth. "The Indo-Caribbean Experience: Now and Then." *Huffington Post,* Dec 6, 2017.

History.com, "Americans overthrow Hawaiian monarchy," February 9, 2010.

Katz, Vikki. "Children as Brokers of Their Immigrant Families' Health-Care Connections," *Social Problems* 61, no. 2: 194 - 215.

Mundy, Liza. "Cracking the Bamboo Ceiling: Can Asian American men learn from *Lean In*?" *The Atlantic*, November 2014.

NYC Mayor's Office for Economic Opportunity, "Poverty Data: Data Tool."

Okamoto, Yoichi. "President Lyndon B. Johnson signs the bill into law as Vice President Hubert Humphrey, Senators Edward M. Kennedy and Robert F. Kennedy and others look on," Wikipedia images, October 3, 1965.

The National Archives, "Japanese-American Internment During World War II," March 17, 2020.

The National Archives Our Documents, "Chinese Exclusion Act (1882)," accessed on March 30, 2020.

Tran, Victoria. "Asian Americans are falling through the cracks in data representation and social services." *Urban Wire* (blog). *The Urban Institute,* June 19, 2018.

UNFPA Asia and the Pacific, "What we do: Population trends," accessed on March 30, 2020.

U.S. Department of Health and Human Services, Office of Minority Health, *Health Disparities Among Pacific Islanders*, by Neal A. Palafox and Momi Kaanoi, Open-file one-pager 2000.

CHAPTER 4: SOLIDARIDAD

Artiga, Samantha, Kendal Orgera, and Anthony Damico, "Changes in Health Coverage by Race and Ethnicity since the ACA, 2010-2018," *Kaiser Family Foundation,* March 5, 2020.

Donovan, Megan K., "EACH Woman Act Offers Bold Path Toward Equitable Abortion Coverage," *Guttmacher Institute,* March 2019.

Gody, Maria. "Dolores Huerta: The Civil Rights Icon Who Showed Farmworkers 'Si Se Puede'." *NPR,* September 17, 2017.

Huey, David. "The US war on drugs and its legacy in Latin America." *The Guardian,* February 3, 2014.

Karmack, Elaine and Christine Stenglein. "How many undocumented immigrants are in the United States and who are they?" *Voter Vitals* (blog). *Brookings Institute,* November 12, 2019.

LinkedIn, "Jessica (Jessica Gonzalez) Gonzalez-Rojas."

Milman, Oliver. "Pesticide that Trump's EPA refused to ban blamed for sickening farm workers." *The Guardian,* May 17, 2017.

National Latina Institute for Reproductive Justice, "Latina Advocacy Networks,"

National Latina Institute for Reproductive Health, "Sin Seguro, No Mas! Without Coverage, No More: Latinx's Access to Abortion Under Hyde," Fact Sheet October 2018. Accessed on May 6, 2020.

National Latina Institute for Reproductive Justice, "Reproductive Justice organizations express dismay that the Hyde amendment was added to the Labor, Health and Human Services, Education, and Related Agencies spending bill," May 8, 2019. Accessed on May 10, 2020.

National Latina Institute for Reproductive Justice, "What We Do."

New American Economy, "Power of the Purse: How Hispanics Contribute to the U.S. Economy," December 2017.

Radford, Jynnah. "Key findings about U.S. immigrants." *Pew Research Center,* June 17, 2019.

United States and who are they?" *Voter Vitals* (blog). *Brookings Institute,* November 12, 2019.

The Dolores Huerta Foundation. "Dolores Huerta." Accessed on April 16, 2020.

Tolbert, Jennifer, Samantha Artiga, and Olivia Pham, "Impact of Shifting Immigration Policy on Medicaid Enrollment and Utilization of Care among Health Center Patients," *Kaiser Family Foundation,* October 15, 2019. Accessed on April 13, 2020.

Tolbert, Jennifer, Kendal Orgera, and Natalie Singer, "Key Facts about the Uninsured Population," *Kaiser Family Foundation,* December 13, 2019. Accessed on May 5, 2020.

Tzalain, Alma Patty. "I Harvest Your Food. Why Isn't My Health 'Essential'?" *The New York Times,* April 15, 2020. Accessed on April 15, 2020.

University of California Berkeley, "DACA Information," June 23, 2020.

U.S. Citizenship and Immigration Services. *Public Charge Fact Sheet,* Washington DC.

U.S. Department of State, Office of the Historian. *Roosevelt Corollary to the Monroe Doctrine, 1904,* Washington DC.

Velasco-Mondragon, Eduardo., "Hispanic health in the USA: a scoping review of the literature," *Public Health Reviews* (2016) 37:31.

"What is Title X? An Explainer," PRH. Accessed on May 9, 2020.

CHAPTER 5: THE AMERICAN HEARTLAND

Baird, Mike and Deanna Larson, "Telehealth's untapped potential in rural America," *Medical Economics,* February 7, 2020. Accessed on May 10, 2020.

Bipartisan Policy Center, "Bipartisan Policy Center."

Bobrow, Emily. "A Midwife in the North Country." *The New Yorker,* December 22, 2019.

Centers for Disease Control, "Drug overdose death rates are higher in rural areas than in urban areas," October 19, 2017. Accessed May 11, 2020.

Centers for Disease Control and Prevention, "Opioid Prescribing Rates in Nonmetropolitan and Metropolitan Counties Among Primary Care Providers Using an Electronic Health Record System -- United States, 2014 - 2017," *Morbidity and Mortality Weekly Report*, January 18, 2019. Accessed on May 11, 2020.

Centers for Disease Control, "Rural Health: About Rural Health." Accessed on May 15, 2020.

Kozhimannil, Katy Backes, Julia D. Interrante, Carrie Henning-Smith, and Lindsay K. Admon, "Rural-Urban Differences in Severe Maternal Morbidity and Mortality in the US, 2007 - 2015," *Health Affairs* 38, no. 12, December 2019.

Madison, Donald. "The Work of James D. Bernstein of North Carolina," *North Carolina Journal of Medicine* 67, no. 1, January/February 2006.

Murthy, Vivek. "Together: The Healing Power of Human Connection in a Sometimes Lonely World." Book website.

Rural Health Information Hub. "Barriers to Telehealth in Rural Areas." Accessed on May 10, 2020.

Rural Health Information Hub, "Chronic Diseases and Condition Prevalence." Accessed on May 10, 2020.

Rural Health Information Hub. "Critical Access Hospitals (CAHs)." Accessed on May 10, 2020.

Sable-Smith, Bram and Wisconsin Public Radio, "Family Doctors In Rural America Tackle Crisis of Addiction and Pain," *Kaiser Health News*, January 10, 2020. Accessed on May 12, 2020.

Searing, Adam. "More Rural Hospitals Closing in States Refusing Medicaid Coverage Expansion." *Rural Health Policy Project*, October 29, 2018.

U.S. Department of Health and Human Services. Health Resources & Services Administration, "NHSC Rural Community Loan Repayment Program." Accessed on May 14, 2020.

Weber, Lauren, "They Enrolled In Medical School To Practice Rural Medicine. What Happened?" *Kaiser Health News*, October 9, 2019. Accessed on May 13, 2020.

CHAPTER 6: HOW THE OTHER HALF LIVES

Blakeman, Bradley. "States are the laboratories of democracy." *The Hill*, May 7, 2020.

Correal, Annie and Andrew Jacobs, "'A Tragedy Is Unfolding': Inside New York's Virus Epicenter," *The New York Times*, April 9, 2020. Updated August 5, 2020.

Gidla, Sujatha. "'We Are Not Essential. We Are Sacrificial." *The New York Times,* May 5, 2020.

Gillespie, Patrick. "Linda Tirado: What I miss about being poor." *CNN Money,* October 2, 2014.

Gorenstein, Dan. "How did we end up with health insurance being tied to our jobs?" *Marketplace,* June 28, 2017.

Harrington, Michael. *The Other America.* New York City: Macmillan Publishers, 1962.

History.com Editors, "Great Society," *History.com*, November 17, 2017.

Khullar, Dhruv and Dave Chokshi, "Health, Income, & Poverty: Where We Are & How We Can Help," *Health Affairs,* October 4, 2018.

Kinja, "Users following Kinja blog."

Luthra, Shefali., "Everything You Need To Know About Block Grants -- The Heart of GOP's Medicaid Plans." *Kaiser Health News,* January 24, 2017.

Markel, Howard. "69 years ago, a president pitches his idea for national health care." *PBS News Hour,* November 19, 2014. Accessed on May 17, 2020.

Medicaid and CHIP Payment and Access Commission, "Changes in coverage and access.

Morrissey, Michael. *Health Insurance: Second Edition.* Chicago: Health Administration Press, 2013.

Seervai, Shanoor, "It's Harder for People Living in Poverty to Get Health Care," *The Commonwealth Fund,* April 19, 2019.

"Status of State Action on the Medicaid Expansion Decision." *Kaiser Family Foundation.*

Stevens, Rosemary. "Health Care in the Early 1960s." *Healthcare Financing Review* 15, no. 2 (1996): 11-22.

Tirado, Linda. "This Is Why Poor People's Bad Decisions Make Perfect Sense." *Huffington Post,* November 22, 2013. Updated December 6, 2017.

Ungar, Laura. "The Deep Divide: State Borders Create Medicaid Haves and Have-Nots." *Kaiser Health News,* October 2, 2019.

U.S. Census Bureau, "Statistical Abstract of the United States: 1962."

U.S. Centers for Medicare and Medicaid Services, Healthcare.gov, "Federal Poverty Level (FPL)," May 2020.

U.S. Centers for Medicare and Medicaid Services, "Medicaid," May 2020. Accessed on May 20, 2020.

U.S. Department of Health & Human Services. Office of the Assistant Secretary for Planning and Evaluation. "Poverty Guidelines," 2020.

van der Voort, Tom. "In The Beginning: Medicare and Medicaid." *UVA Miller Center,* July 24, 2017.

Williamson, Alanna, Larisa Antonisse, Jennifer Tolbert, Rachel Garfield, and Anthony Damico. "ACA Coverage Expansions and Low-Income Workers." *Kaiser Family Foundation,* June 10, 2016.

Wright, D.K. "West Virginia woman's plea to Congress makes national news." *ABC 4,* February 13, 2020.

CHAPTER 7: THE "FAIRER SEX"

Amazon. "Obstacle Course: The Everyday Struggle to Get an Abortion in America."

Consumer Reports. "Is bias keeping female, minority patients from getting proper care for their pain?" *The Washington Post,* July 29, 2019.

Dusenbery, Maya. "'All In Your Head?' Getting Care for Untreated Pain." *Consumer Reports,* May 2, 2019.

Dusenbery, Maya. "Compared to Men, Women Bear Six Times More of the Cost of Alzheimer's Disease." *Pacific Standard,* June 14, 2017.

Goodreads, "Aristotle > Quotes."

Greenwood, Brad N., Seth Carnahan, and Laura Huang, "Patient-physician gender concordance and increased mortality among female heart attack patients," *Proceedings of the*

National Academy of Sciences of the United States of America 115, no. 24 (2018): 8569-8574.

Gross, Terry. "How 'Bad Medicine' Dismisses And Misdiagnoses Women's Symptoms." March 27, 2018. In *Fresh Air*. Produced by Heidi Saman and Seth Kelley. Podcast, MP3 audio, 19:17.

Jackson, Gabrielle. "The female problem: how male bias in medical trials ruined women's health." *The Guardian,* November 13, 2019.

Moore, Anna. "Why does medicine treat women like men?" *The Guardian,* May 24, 2020.

Nerenberg, Jenara. "How to Address Gender Inequality in Health Care." *Greater Good Magazine.* March 9, 2018.

Paulsen, Emily. "Recognizing, Addressing Unintended Gender Bias in Patient Care." *Duke Health*, October 9, 2019.

Pollitt, Katha. "The long fight for reproductive rights is only getting harder." *The Washington Post,* May 13, 2020.

The Shriver Report. "A Woman's Nation Takes On Alzheimer's." October 2010.

Trevino, Julissa, "New Paper Examines How Gender Bias in Health Care Can Be Deadly." *Rewire.News,* October 4, 2018.

CHAPTER 8: HERE, QUEER & WITHOUT FEAR

"A pink triangle against a black backdrop with the words 'Silence = Death' representing an advertisement for the Silence = Death Project used by permission by ACT-UP, The AIDS Coalition to Unleash Power. Colour lithograph, 1987." *Wellcome Collection.*

"ACT UP," *ACT UP* website.

Dowd, Maureen. "For Victims of AIDS, Support in a Lonely Siege," *The New York Times.* December 5, 1983.

Fitzsimmons, Tim. "LGBTQ History Month: The early days of America's AIDS crisis." *NBC News.* October 15, 2018.

Garg, Ananya. "What Cities Are Doing to Help Trans Women of Color," *CityLab.* March 27, 2020.

"GMHC: End AIDS. Live Life," *Gay Men's Health Crisis* website.

Grant, Jaime, Lisa Mottet, Justin Tanis, Jack Harrison, Jody Herman, and Mara Keisling, "Injustice at Every Turn: A Report of the National Transgender Discrimination Survey," *National Center for Transgender Equality,* September 2012.

Greytak, Emily, Joseph G. Kosciw, Christian Villenas, and Noreen M. Giga, "From Teasing to Torment: School Climate Revisited," *GLSEN,* 2016.

Hafeez, Hudaisa, Muhammad Zeshan, Muhammad A. Tahir, Nusrat Jahan, and Sadiq Naveed, "Health Care Disparities Among Lesbian, Gay, Bisexual, and Transgender Youth: A Literature Review," *Cureus* 9, no. 4 (2017): 1-7.

Harvard Business School, "Perspectives: Soltan Bryce, MBA 2021."

Lawson, Richard. "The Reagan administration's unearthed response to the AIDS crisis is chilling," *Vanity Fair.* December 1, 2015.

Leland, John. "Twilight of a Difficult Man: Larry Kramer and the Birth of AIDS Activism," *The New York Times.* May 19, 2017.

Maxouris, Christina. "Marsha P. Johnson, a black transgender woman, was a central figure in the gay liberation movement," *CNN.* June 26, 2019.

National LGBT Health Education Center. "Learning to Address Implicit Bias Towards LGBTQ Patients: Case Scenarios." September 2018.

Nobel, Jeremy. "Finding Connection Through 'Chosen Family,'" *Psychology Today.* June 14, 2019.

Peters, Jeremy. "A Conservative Push to Make Trans Kids and School Sports the Next Battleground in the Culture War," *The New York Times.* August 18, 2020.

Shaw, Maggie. "FDA's Revised Blood Donation Guidance for Gay Men Still Courts Controversy," *American Journal of Managed Care.* April 4, 2020.

Simmons-Duffin, Selena. "Transgender Health Protections Reversed By Trump Administration," *NPR.* June 12, 2020.

"Stonewall Riots." *History.com*, June 26, 2020.

U.S. Centers for Disease Control and Prevention. "About HIV," July 14, 2020.

U.S. Centers for Disease Control. "HIV: Gay and Bisexual Men."

U.S. Centers for Disease Control and Prevention. "Sex Workers." August 2016.

Walsh, Katie. "Review: A 72-year lesbian romance for the ages revealed in 'A Secret Love'," *LA Times.* May 1, 2020.

"You Don't Want Second Best: Anti-LGBT Discrimination in US Health Care." *Human Rights Watch.* 2018.

Yong, Ed, "Young Trans Children Know Who They Are," *The Atlantic*, January 15, 2019.

Zraick, Karen. "Texas Father Says 7-Year Old Isn't Transgender, Igniting a Politicized Outcry," *The New York Times.* October 28, 2019.

CHAPTER 9: BEYOND BUZZWORDS

Alexander, Julia. "YouTube's BetterHelp mental health controversy, explained." *Polygon*, October 4, 2018.

Angwin, Julia, Jeff Larson, Surya Mattu, and Lauren Kirchnere, "Machine Bias," *ProPublica,* May 23, 2016.

Beam Health website.

Plume website.

Flores, Andrew, Jody Herman, Gary Gates, and Taylor Brown, "How Many Adults Identify as Transgender in the United States?" *UCLA School of Law Williams Institute,* June 2016.

Gawande, Atul. "Why Doctors Hate Their Computers." *The New Yorker,* November 5, 2018.

"Healthie's Mission," *Healthie.com* website.

HMS Health Ideas Staff. "Social Determinants of Health: The Impact on Members, Health

Kangovi, Shreya, Nandita Mitra, David Grande, Judith A. Long, and David A. Asch. "Evidence-Based Community Health Worker Program Addresses Unmet Social Needs And Generates Positive Return On Investment: A return on investment analysis of a randomized controlled trial of a standardized community health worker program that addresses unmet social needs for disadvantaged individuals." *Health Affairs* 39, no. 2 (2020): 207-213.

Outcomes and the Bottom Line," *Modern Healthcare.* March 6, 2019.

Plume staff. "Why Plume?", *Plume.com* website. May 27, 2020.

Rogers, Katie. "BREAKING: Planned Parenthood defunded from the Title X Program." *Planned Parenthood of Indiana and Kentucky Inc.,* August 19, 2019.

"Who is Healthify?" *Healthify.com* website.

CHAPTER 10: STANDING ON THE SHOULDERS OF GIANTS

Abrams, Abigail. "The Surprising Origins of 'Medicare for All.'" *TIME,* May 30, 2019.

"Approval of syringe exchange programs in California: results from a local approach to HIV prevention." *American Journal of Public Health* 98, no. 2 (2008): 278-283.

Bluthenthal, Ricky, Keith Heinzerling, Rachel Anderson, Neil Flynn, and Alex Kral, "Approval of Syringe Exchange Programs in California: Results From a Local Approach to HIV Prevention," *American Journal of Public Health* 98, no. 2 (2008): 278-283.

Caruso, Dominic, David Himmelstein, Steffie Woolhandler, "Single-Payer Health Reform: A Step Toward Reducing Structural Racism in Health Care," *Harvard Public Health Review* no. 7 (2015): 1-4.

Collins, Sara, Herman Bhupal, and Michelle Doty. "Health Insurance Coverage Eight Years After the ACA." *The Commonwealth Fund,* February 7, 2019.

Diamond, Dan. "Pulse Check: 'Harry and Louise'—and Hillary," *POLITICO,* May 12, 2016.

"Evolent Health and SOMOS IPA Aim to Provide Physician-Driven Medicaid Managed Care through New York Innovator Program." *CISION PR Newswire,* November 6, 2018.

Jacobs, Emma. "Needle Exchange Program Creates Black Market in Clean Syringes," *NPR*. January 3, 2015.

James, Scott. "A Life Devoted to Health, Framed by His Siblings' Disabilities," *The New York Times*. December 16, 2010.

Kacik, Alex. "Monopolized healthcare market reduces quality, increases costs," *Modern Healthcare*, April 13, 2017.

Katz, Mitchell. "What the US healthcare system assumes about you." Filmed November 2018 in Palm Springs, CA. TEDMED video, 15:52.

Klausner, Jeffrey, Charlotte Kent, William Wong, Jacque McCright, and Mitchell Katz, "The Public Health Response to Epidemic Syphilis, San Francisco, 1999-2004," *Sexually Transmitted Diseases* 32, no. 10 (2005): S11-S18.

Murad, Yusra. "As Coronavirus Surges, 'Medicare for All' Supports Hits 9-Month High." *Morning Consult,* April 1, 2020.

"Pharmacy Benefit Managers and Their Role in Drug Spending." *The Commonwealth Fund,* April 22, 2019.

SOMOS website.

Soni, Aparna, Laura Wherry, and Kosali Simon, "How Have ACA Insurance Expansions Affected Health Outcomes? Findings From The Literature." *Health Affairs* 39, no. 3 (2020).

Verma, Seema. "Thank Obamacare for the Rise of the Uninsured," *CMS.gov,* September 13, 2019.

CHAPTER 11: LOOKING TO THE PAST TO UNDERSTAND THE FUTURE

"Agricultural Worker Demographics." *National Center for Farmworker Health, Inc.,* 2018.

Korcok, Milan. "Canada's single-payer healthcare system—a system in turbulence, but beloved nonetheless." *International Travel & Health Insurance Journal,* February 3, 2020.

Kottasová, Ivana. "Britain's health service is part of its national psyche. It's also on life support." *CNN,* April 18, 2020.

Kuttner, Robert. "A Conversation with Doris Kearns Goodwin." *The American Prospect,* December 17, 2007.

Porter, Eduardo. "Why America Will Never Get Medicare for All." *The New York Times,* March 14, 2020.

Tzalain, Alma Patty. "I Harvest Your Food. Why Isn't My Health 'Essential'?" *The New York Times,* April 15, 2020. Accessed on April 15, 2020.

CHAPTER 12: HEALTH CARE PROFILES IN COURAGE

Borrelli, Christopher. "Reagan used her, the country hated her. Decades later, the Welfare Queen of Chicago refuses to go away." *Chicago Tribune,* June 10, 2019.

Burke-Harris, Nadine. "How childhood trauma affects health across a lifetime." Filmed November 2014 in San Francisco, CA. TEDMED video, 15:51.

Delbanco, Suzanne, Maclaine Lehan, Thi Montalvo, and Jeffrey Levin-Scherz, "The Rising U.S. Maternal Mortality Rate Demands Action from Employers," *Harvard Business Review,* June 28, 2019.

Fetters, Ashley. "The Doctor Doesn't Listen to Her. But the Media is Starting To." *The Atlantic,* August 10, 2018.

"Jim Crow Museum of Racist Memorabilia: The Sapphire Caricature," *Ferris State University,* 2012.

Little, Katrina. "The Dying Mothers, Sisters, Daughters, Friends," Filmed September 2019 in Denver, CO. TEDxMSUDenver video, 13:50.

Mitropolous, Arielle and Mariya Moseley, "Beloved Brooklyn Teacher, 30, diees of coronavirus after she was twice denied a COVID-19 test," *ABC News,* April 28, 2020.

Musumeci, MaryBeth. "Explaining California v. Texas: A Guide to the Case Challenging the ACA." *Kaiser Family Foundation,* September 1, 2020.

Patel, Rhea. "Walmart and Oak Street Health launch joint health clinics." *Business Insider,* September 4, 2020.

Salam, Maya. "For Serena Williams, Childbirth Was a Harrowing Ordeal. She's Not Alone." *The New York Times,* January 11, 2018.

"The Color of Law: A Forgotten History of How Our Government Segregated America." *Economic Policy Institute,* 2017.

Vedantam, Shankar, Jennifer Schmidt, Parth Shah, Tara Boyle, and
Rhaina Cohen. "People Like Us: How Our Identities Shape
Health And Educational Success." June 3, 2019 in *Hidden Brain*,
produced by NPR, MP3 audio, 35:24.

CHAPTER 13: AN ODE

Aasland, Dan. "Protesters in Minneapolis, Minnesota where
George Floyed was killed and the unrest began." Wikipedia
images, May 29, 2020.

Alperin, Elijah and Jeanne Batalova. "Vietnamese Immigrants
in the United States." *Migration Policy Institute,* September
13, 2018.

Bhattaral, Abha. "Retail workers are being pulled into the latest
culture war: Getting customers to wear masks," *The Washington Post,* July 8, 2020.

Bichell, Rae Ellen. "Scientists Start to Tease Out The Subtler Ways
Racism Hurts Health." *NPR,* November 11, 2017.

Dall, Chris. "As pandemic rages, PPE supply remains a problem." *Center for Infectious Disease and Research Policy News*,
July 29, 2020.

Dickerson, Caitlin and Miriam Jordan, "South Dakota Meat Plant
Is Now Country's Biggest Coronavirus Hot Spot." *The New
York Times,* May 4, 2020.

"Double Jeopardy: COVID-19 and Behavioral Health Disparities for Black and Latino Communities in the U.S." *Substance Abuse and Mental Health Services Administration,* 2020.

Emma. "The gender wars of household chores: a feminist comic." *The Guardian,* May 26, 2017.

Healy, Jack and Serge Kovaleski."The Coronavirus's Rampage Through a Suburban Nursing Home." *The New York Times,* May 21, 2020.

Jeffery, Adam. "New Yorkers stop and give daily thanks and gratitude for coronavirus frontline workers." *CNBC,* April 10, 2020.

Joseph, Andrew. "'We don't actually have that answer yet': WHO clarifies comments on asymptomatic spread of Covid-19." *Stat,* June 9, 2020.

Knoll, Corina, Ali Watkins, and Michaeel Rothfeld. "'I Couldn't Do Anything': The Virus and an E.R. Doctor's Suicide." *The New York Times,* July 11, 2020.

Lee, Matthew. "Coronavirus fears show how 'model minority' Asian Americans become the 'yellow peril.'" *NBC,* March 9, 2020.

Levenson, Eric."Why New York is the epicenter of the American coronavirus outbreak. *CNN,* March 26, 2020.

Office of Governor Gavin Newsom. "Governor Gavin Newsom Issues Stay at Home Order." *CA.gov,* March 19, 2020.

"Pupils at Carlisle Indian Industrial School, Pennsylvania (c.1900," Public Domain, September 16, 2008.

"Racial Trauma." *Mental Health America* website, June 25, 2020.

The Editors. "Too Many Black Americans Are Dying from COVID-19." *Scientific American,* August 1, 2020.

The New York Times. "Block by Block: Jackson Heights." *The New York Times,* November 17, 2015.

Travers, Karen and Jordyn Phelps. "Trump using daily crisis briefings to stay in the political spotlight." *ABC News,* April 9, 2020.

Tzalain, Alma Patty. "I Harvest Your Food. Why Isn't My Health 'Essential'?" *The New York Times,* April 15, 2020.

Wu, Katherine. "C.D.C. Now Says People Without Covid-19 Symptoms Do Not Need Testing." *The New York Times,* September 17, 2020.

CPSIA information can be obtained
at www.ICGtesting.com
Printed in the USA
BVHW041944220221
600811BV00016B/425

9 781636 765082